The Language of Discipline

A Practical Approach to Effective Classroom Management

William A. Rogers

BTh (Hons), DipMin, DipTeach, BEd (Melb)
MEd (Melb), MACE

Northcote House

First published in 1994 by Northcote House Publishers Ltd, Plymbridge House, Estover Road, Plymouth PL6 7PZ, United Kingdom. Tel: Plymouth (0752) 695745/ 735251 Fax: (0752) 695699. Telex: 45635.

British Library Cataloguing-in-Publication Data

A catalogue record for this book is available from the British Library.

ISBN 0-7463-0651-2

Typeset by PDQ Typesetting, Stoke-on-Trent
Printed and bound by BPCC Wheatons Ltd, Exeter

Contents

Preface

I finished this book while conducting a summer school at Cambridge University (during a Melbourne winter). This is the third summer school I've taken with teachers coming from all over England (some from Europe) to explore discipline skills, teacher stress, developing positive behaviours with students and developing whole-school approaches to student behaviour management. The issues they raised, the concerns and problems they had with discipline, were no different from those of Australian teachers:

- children who are aware of, and vocal, about their rights
- challenging and argumentative behaviour
- the natural stresses created by a multi-task role
- children with socio-emotional problems

I've worked in many UK schools now (taking INSET) and for many LEAs on issues related to school discipline and have noted a movement away from punitive approaches to more positive, whole-school approaches consistent with a rights–responsibility focus.

The *Independent* newspaper ran a series of articles in July 1992 on what it called 'The best schools in Britain'. As each school summarised its ethos and practice, discipline was often referred to with descriptions such as 'firm but fair', 'positive and relaxed', 'good personal relationships', 'even the sanctions have a nice flavour' (5 July 1992 p.43), 'self-control', 'personal responsibility and self-discipline', 'purpose and order'.

This book is an attempt to put 'flesh' on those desirable 'bones'.

Balancing rights and responsibilities in schools requires different skills of teachers today. The effective teacher is not merely the one who can keep the class quiet and under control by dint of threat, reprimand, guilt or fear. These days teachers need a more skilled approach to discipline and classroom management, one that recognises the need to work with students; to accept the need for fundamental rights including the right of reply, the right to participate in decisions that affect them, the right to be treated as a *social* equal, not as inferior subordinates but with dignity and justice.

This does not mean a return to some of the democratic experiments of the 1970s but rather an approach that balances the fundamental three Rs — rights, responsibilities and rules — in the context of behaviour ownership, participation in the social *and* learning life of the group, respect for others, positive working relationships and enhanced self-esteem. This book addresses the skills effective teachers use to manage disruptive behaviour in the present context. The emphasis is on the concept of planning our discipline and management, especially the **language of discipline**. Discipline is one of the more stressful aspects of our demanding role. It needs acute planning and skill as well as 'a personality' that lends itself to a role that operates in a relational context. It's helpful, of course, if you actually like working with young people!

One of the key skills in this book is that of assertion, how we use discipline language in addressing disruptive behaviour, how we can avoid the often pointless (and emotionally taxing) power struggles and how we can be 'economic' in dealing with disruptive behaviour.

Children need 'discipline' for their own and others' security, discipline expressed as the teacher's leadership to enable a student to move towards self-discipline. When discipline is effective the teacher is making possible the maximum enjoyment of the due rights of all (including the teacher's fundamental right to teach) by *enabling* students to meet their responsibilities — no mean feat.

This book sets out a skills programme at the classroom and school level that seeks to meet those goals within the bounds of creative fallibility.

William A. Rogers
September 1993

Acknowledgements

It's hard to believe a writer would still hand-write these days. I do. I heartily thank, therefore, Joy Draper and Jenni Shields for the ability to translate my handwriting into presentable prose.

I thank the many teachers who have allowed me to work in their rooms with them, and those who watched me take many demonstration classes. I've learned much from their feedback as I trust they have from mine.

It's difficult writing a book from Australia to England and I have appreciated the goodwill and support of the publishers and especially Brian Hulme.

Lastly thanks to Lora (my wife) for her patience and feedback (Lora is a teacher too). We've both used these skills as teachers and in a modified way with our all-knowing, but great, children.

Introduction

THE LANGUAGE OF DISCIPLINE

Teachers daily have to address a wide range of student misbehaviour. It is a taxing feature of a demanding profession — helping students to own their behaviour, be responsible, respect the rights of others.

A key feature of this text is its focus on **language** as a primary tool in creating a workable relationship between teacher and students. Most discipline is a balance of what we say (**content**), when we say it (**timing**) and how we say it (**tone**). Of course, language, without a serviceable working relationship, would be mere technique. This book is concerned with how in practice to balance building a positive relationship with the need to discipline. The emphasis throughout is on skills one can learn to enhance a discipline style based on respect and dignity without sacrificing appropriate assertion.

As you work through the text you'll come across many teacher (T) and student (S) dialogues. Attention is drawn to the effect of what we say and how we say it as teachers. As you read these dialogues imagine yourself in the room, twenty-five odd eyes and ears listening, watching. Try saying the dialogues in different tones — fun tone, hostile tone, sarcastic tone, aggressive tone, sycophantic-indecisive tone (pleading) — and work on a firm, pleasant, assertive tone. Students pick up largely on how we say something as well as what we say.

Because discipline often occurs in an emotionally affected setting, our discipline language is more effective when it is planned rather than left to chance. This is the theme of this book, a conscious repertoire planned ahead of time so that we can deal more effectively, and economically, with 'the thousand natural shocks that flesh is heir to' (Shakespeare, *Hamlet*).

WHAT DO I DO WHEN...?

I take demonstration classes (masochism, heroism, stupidity?) — one of my colleagues calls it the world's cheapest enema. Taking lessons while other teachers watch, though, has taught me a lot about teaching, management, students, myself.... My colleagues and I use it as part of a peer-coaching programme.

A year 10 class: I walk into the room as thirty-two 14 and 15 year-olds file in noisily. Two teachers are already ensconced at the back waiting to observe the lesson. I've been warned about a few customers: Ben, Neil and Mark; and watch Vanessa. That helps me no end!

Ben takes the back left seat with a coterie of friends, grinning, with 'What's this then?' and 'Who's he anyway?' looks. Vanessa is leaning back in heavy chair lean mode and having a 'two bob each way' chat with her friend while checking me out. There is the ritual settling noise. I notice as I 'start' a couple of mouths chewing. Normal. It's establishment phase. Natural testing time. They need to sort out (for themselves) what this teacher is like.

'Morning, I'll be taking this class today. My name's Mr Rogers. I don't know you all; a quick whip around with the names....' As I get feedback on the names I see a small rubber ball parabolically aimed at, and hitting, the blackboard. It bounces off on to the floor near my feet. What do I do? I see Vanessa leaning back talking to Lisa. What do I do? The gum-chewers? Craig has his foot (his large Reebok foot) on the desk and is seat leaning.

Neil calls out, clicking his fingers. What do I do? He later says, 'Can I go to the toilet?' (during instruction time). Do I let him go? It is a highly public setting. Several of the students are after 'street credibility' — a pecking order of 'belonging'. Whatever I do I need to be aware of the social dynamics as well as what I'm teaching; to be aware of the discipline I give, and avoid silly win/lose power struggles. 'What do I do, say, and when?' and 'What happens if what I do doesn't work?' are valid questions. I have to juggle my own emotions with my discipline and their reactions.

What if I *say*, for example, 'Right!! Who threw that, come on, who threw it?! Was it you, yes, you down the back, Ben isn't it?' 'Me?!' he feigns.

Let's say I walk up to Ben (I *think* it was he who threw the ball — aiming for the bin) with shoulders tense, chin out, fists clenched, the racing thought 'I'll maim that little acronym'. I telegraph via my body language that it's a threat. If I then say, 'Right, it was you, wasn't it — why did you do that?! Eh?!' He might reply, 'Wasn't me?!' (Here he'll look around at his coterie for support — the Greek chorus says 'yeah!' — 'Shut up you — I wasn't talking to you!') 'C'mon, you, yes you Ben isn't it? Pick it up!' 'Told yer I didn't throw it, what you picking on me for?!'

This approach is based on win/lose, high status and is often doomed to failure as each 'side' vies for emotional and verbal supremacy. It arises from strong cognitive demands (and beliefs) that children *must* respect their teachers and *must* do as they're told — whatever.

'You, get that gum in the bin!' If the teacher walks over, especially during up-front, instructional time, on a 'small beer' issue like this and acts and speaks confrontationally, is it any wonder the 'secondary' behaviour of the students is a 'lie'? 'Wasn't chewing,' 'Don't lie to me — get it in the bin!' 'I was just chewing me tongue — get real!' 'Don't-you-speak-to-me-in-that-tone-of-voice!' (The teacher speaks in a 'machine gun' voice.) All this, over chewing gum.

T   You, yes you, Vanessa and Lisa, don't talk while I'm teaching!
Ss   We were only [said with a pouting, curled lip, arms folded, sneer] talking about the work! [hurt sigh to finish off the 'effect']. These students are seeking to gain some public attention — ['Notice me!']
T   [Walks up close.] Don't con me. You were not talking about the work at all — do you think I'm stupid or what?! [Here they grin.] And wipe that smirk off your face.
Ss   Anyway, watchya picking on us for? Ben 'n Daniel were talking before, didn't say nothing to them. No *they're* boys! [here Lisa tosses her head.]

By this time the teacher is getting close to terminal frustration mode. Anything can happen. He believes he has to control all these incidents *directly*, but each time he speaks, and the way he speaks, is feeding a self-defeating cycle.

Attempting to control
There are a number of characteristic teacher behaviours that flow from teachers believing that it is in their direct power to control, by fiat:

- *They* tend to take on all the responsibility for the child's behaviour.
- The verb 'to make' is applied to their methods of 'control'. 'I'll make him do as he's told.' A belief that 'I can force him to obey me!'
- They minimise 'choice' or appropriate negotiation.
- They get locked into self-defeating power struggles.
- They use hostility, sarcasm, 'bolshie' tactics. They will not allow appropriate 'face-saving' for the student and will resort to 'public' embarrassment. If there is one thing students hate it is being

directly put down in front of their peers.

Of course, these teachers, in 'safe' schools, may still get results through obedience based on a fear–compliance approach. They also get rebellion, resentment, alienation, defiance.

In a day and age when students believe they are our social equal this force method is increasingly failing to work. But even it does, is such an approach right? (A value question).

There are also teachers who discipline in this way because they get so frustrated by students answering back and having the last word. Because emotion, beliefs and behaviour are so intertwined, reactive discipline styles go on being repeated and become self-justifying.

Non-assertion

Conversely there are teachers who have unclear expectations, uncertain, unclear and poorly enforced rules. Such teachers have difficulty asserting their rights as teachers. Their voice tone and body language may convey that they are threatened. They *look* passive, anxious, uncertain of where they are going. In a conflict situation they often allow children to dominate by useless discussion of secondary issues (Rogers 1991b, 1992a, 1992b).

T   Daniel, come on please, put the chewing gum into the bin. [His voice implies, 'I don't expect you to do this, but I really hope you will and I don't want you to dislike me but it is a rule....']

S   C'mon Sir, get real, s'only a bit of gum. I'm still doing my work! [Hurt tone as if to say 'you're most unfair to address a minor issue like this!]

T   But Daniel it's the rule [rising inflection, hands outstretched, wrinkled brow], please put it in the bin.

S   [Student butts in] But other teachers here let us chew gum, don't they? [Here Daniel appeals to the supportive chorus. 'Yeah!' says Rob folding his arms in closed body language. It's a 'social-justice' issue now involving other students.]

T   Oh, c'mon Rob, which teachers let you eat chewing gum in class? [So it goes on — the side issues beginning to take over.]

Back to Ben and co.

OK. What in fact did I do? I picked up the ball *while* I was talking to the class *as if* it was no big deal, dropped it in the bin and carried on instructional time. After all, I wasn't certain Ben had thrown it.

I could have used many approaches depending on:

- My beliefs and attitudes about the nature of power and control
- How threatened I felt
- What my skill repertoire in discipline was
- How well I felt on the day
- My understanding of group dynamics
- How well I had planned my discipline (the key theme of this book)

I could have used humour, a powerful defuser: 'Poor shot [wink] I'll discuss tactics after class', then confidently resume the lesson flow.

What about Craig with his foot up? What if I walk up and make a scene? 'Do you put your feet on the furniture at home!' 'Yeah, was only resting it [smirk]!' He may well put his feet up at home. I got a better response by just using directional language:

T   Craig [eye contact — without moving too close when 'up-front'] feet down, thanks, and facing this way.

The tone is relaxed, expectant and moving on with the lesson *as if* he'll do it. If he doesn't I'll repeat and redirect but not argue (see pp. 87-9).

Same with the two girls talking.

T   Vanessa and Lisa [establish eye contact] facing this way and listening thank you. [Firm, pleasant, with an 'as if' tone.]
Ss   We're only talking about the work!
T   [*Tactically*, ignore the tone and refuse to get drawn into the 'secondary' issues. Redirect to the primary issue.] Maybe you were but I want you to face the front and listen thanks.

Resume the flow of the lesson, in control, not of the two girls, but of the lesson, allowing Lisa and Vanessa take-up time and enabling them not to lose face. When we *overdwell* (Kounin 1971) on secondary issues we break the 'flow'.

PLAN FOR EFFECTIVE DISCIPLINE

The point is I cannot effectively discipline if I don't have a plan. This plan has to take into account four major aspects of discipline (see Fig.1): preventative, corrective, consequential and supportive (repair and rebuild). Effective discipline balances these four essential areas.

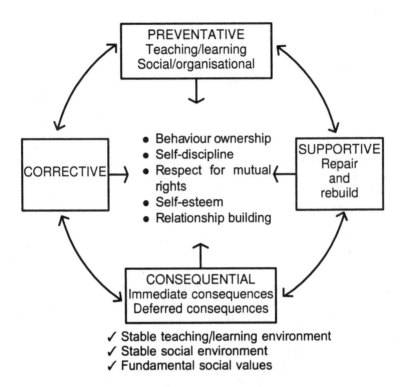

Fig. 1. The four phases of discipline

Preventative

This covers aspects of the classroom such as lesson planning, both the units of work and individual lessons: catering for mixed abilities; thinking about the seating and aesthetics in the room (air flow from windows, movement flow around the room, carpet helps noise level, fix any broken furniture quickly, lighting); communicating routines (for work, monitors, toilet procedures, packing up); and planning a language of discipline prior to the need to use it. It's difficult to know what to say *when* we're under emotional pressure. A plan can help. We know (as research confirms: Elton 1989, Rogers 1992a) that teachers rate calling out, talking out of turn, argumentative (and the 'last word' syndrome) students, seat-wandering and task avoidance as their major disruptions. While these are not serious it's the frequency of the behaviour that is so frustrating.

Effective management, and discipline, is a matter not merely of personality or good fortune but of skill:

> The most talented 'natural' teachers may need little training or advice because they learn so quickly from experience. At the other extreme, there are few teachers for whom training and advice will not be properly effective because their personalities do not match the needs of the job. It is clear, however, that the majority of teachers can become more effective classroom managers as a result of the right kinds of training, experience and support.
>
> *The Elton Report,* p. 69

Be aware of group dynamics and some of the games students play, especially the secondary behaviour game (see pp. 25-31).

It is also essential to make the classroom 'rules' or 'agreements' clear in the establishment phase of your time with the group. Fair, clear and 'owned' rules help protect the rights of all and give a basis for corrective discipline where necessary.

Corrective
However well we plan for a lesson, there will be minor disruptions such as calling out, chit-chat, off-task behaviours. In 'difficult' schools there will be regular bouts of clowning, teacher-baiting, task avoidance and task refusal.

An effective principle of discipline is to begin at the least intrusive level and only move to the most intrusive as the situation, context and circumstance necessitate. For example David has sneaked his Walkman cassette recorder into class.

T   Right! [Teacher walks over, heavy footed, hand outstretched]. Give it to me! Come on, hand it over!

S   Come on, I didn't have it on!

T   I don't care, hand it over.

S   No way, I'm not doing anything wrong.

This the most intrusive stance *invites* a power struggle and with some students offers them, on a plate, the win/lose game they may be looking for.

A least intrusive stance sees the teacher walk quietly over, establish eye contact (smiles are even appropriate), after all it's not a major crime! and say in a firm but calm voice:

T   David, nice Walkman. [This *prefaces* the discipline direction you're about to give, it makes it more difficult for the student to dislike you]. You know the school rule. [Rule reminder] Put the Walkman in your bag or on my desk, thank you.

S　　Oh, come on, Miss Snaggs in art lets us have them on! [A sulky pout appears.]

T　　[Instead of arguing, 'I don't care if every teacher in the school lets you have it, WHAT DID I SAY?!!' — the teacher redirects.] Maybe she does but the rule is clear. In your bag or on my desk, thanks. [At this point the teacher walks away from David as if he'll do it, allowing take-up time and some 'face-saving'.]

If David refuses to put his Walkman away in class (most will comply) I can hardly *just* make him. If I go to snatch it and a counter-grab plus verbal heat is exchanged, what's the point? Win/lose confrontations only service power exchanges. I can walk away leaving David to own his 'choice', to put it in his bag or on my desk, or he can face a deferred consequence. All my ranting or pleading (in front of the class audience) won't change his attitude.

'Dave, if you continue to keep it on your desk, I'll have to follow it up later — after class.' The 'tribal tom-toms' of the group will soon know that the deferred consequence was carried out.

By using the least intrusive measures (directional choices, casual and direct questions, reminders, encouragement, distraction and diversion, privately understood signals, redirections) teachers can keep transactional heat down and increase the likelihood of behaviour ownership in the student.

This is not merely words either. The teacher's tone is pleasant but assertive, the eye contact is established, but the ball is in the student's court. If he refuses this reminder/'choice' the teacher can come back with a consequence statement (see below). Each intervention by the teacher is reminding without arguing that the student is required to own his (or her) own behaviour and respect others' rights in that room. It is the reasonable consistency of a teacher's daily corrective style that will communicate fairness, assertion and care: the language of discipline.

The elements of corrective discipline are discussed in detail in Chapter 4, with applications to common disruptive behaviours.

Consequential

If the students refuse to own their behaviour they will be faced with 'choosing' a consequence. Students need to be treated as if they can 'choose' consequences. To do that they need to know the fair rules, and the positive rights behind those rules. They also need encouragement and positive reinforcement when they work by the fair rules. If students choose to resist the rules they need to face the reasonable consequences.

Supportive

Finally supportive discipline completes the cycle. When any consequence has been carried through it is important to re-establish a working relationship between teacher and student, to repair emotional breaches. With repeatedly disruptive student behaviour the teacher (with peer support) will need to work on a longer term plan (beyond consequences) to repair and rebuild dysfunctional patterns of behaviour.

LEADERSHIP, NOT CONTROL

Traditionally the word discipline has concentrated on punishment and control, often couched in combative metaphors. Schools have a history of corporal (physical) punishment, canes, straps, ear-pulling, hair-pulling, shoving, finger-poking-in-shoulder, public embarrassment – even humiliation. In the mid-1980s, in most democratic countries, the cane (*et al.*) was abolished. Nowadays the emphasis is on self-discipline rather than teacher control.

I prefer to use the concept of *discipline leadership* rather than 'control'. *How* can we lead, guide, direct, encourage, remind, teach and (sometimes) assert and confront students to:

- 'own' their own behaviour, accept responsibility for their behaviour, and accept accountability for their behaviour?
- respect the fundamental rights of others to be safe, feel safe, learn and be treated with respect?
- embrace fundamental values of honesty, a fair-go, the dignity of the person?
- co-operate in a group (classroom and wider school community)?
- believe in themselves?
- value themselves (self-esteem)?
- gain the best they can from their schooling experience?

The *way* we daily guide, lead, teach is in effect part of the discipline process that seeks to reach these goals. Ambitious!

Rather than merely control the student we are asking: how can I set up the classroom (and the school), how can I manage and discipline, so that the goals outlined above can be realised in any meaningful way? Discipline, then, under this definition is what I say and do on a *characteristic* basis, that enables the student/s to embrace those goals.

Having a discipline plan

To do this in any effective way we need to recognise the need for a plan. The major emphasis of this book is that if discipline is going to be effective it needs to be planned. The goals mentioned above will rarely be met by accident; fortuitously. Like most things in teaching *effective* discipline needs planning.

Few teachers go into class without a lesson plan (of some sort), yet I've worked with and met significant numbers of teachers who will walk into calling out, butting in, seat-wandering, procrastination, argumentative students, task avoidance and so on — without a discipline plan.

A discipline plan embraces the four aspects of management mentioned earlier: preventative, corrective, consequential and supportive.

Central to this discipline, management and teaching process are fundamental **values** we hold about dignity, human worth, the way we treat individuals in our society (the Judaeo-Christian heritage on which these values are built). **Human rights** are fundamental expectations arising from those values. **Rules** are social constraints designed, within the group, to bring some protection of those rights and indicate responsibilities and duties with respect to those rights. **Consequences** are the way the group brings accountability to bear upon those individuals who affect, or abuse, others' rights.

Bringing natural justice to bear on these elements is never easy. In the Western tradition the balance of freedom and responsibilities is addressed by a framework of rights, responsibilities, rules and consequences.

1

Disruptive Behaviour

In any class, on average, teachers can expect some approximation to the 'normal curve' when it comes to disruptive behaviour. About 80 per cent of the class (and the school) will be reasonably on-task, co-operative, responsible, working by the rules. Perhaps 15 per cent will make life difficult by their testing, challenging, attention-seeking behaviour; like the rest of the class, though, positive and fair discipline coupled with a spirited attempt at a curriculum matched to ability and need will win through. It's a harder slog with the 15 per cent that's all. Up to 5 per cent will be significantly disruptive — these are students who drain the emotional life of teachers by the frequency and intensity of their disruptive behaviour (Wragg 1989, Rogers 1992b). Disruptive behaviour is a normal (even natural) feature of school life. Any institution reflecting (as schools do) the social mix they serve will, obviously, reflect social mores, values and behaviour patterns. In the classroom this will be seen in 'low level' (but nuisance) disruptions such as calling out, fidgeting, talking out of turn and butting in, distracting noises (shuffling, pen-tapping, fiddling, etc.), task avoidance, heavy-weather seat-leaners — or more disturbing behaviours such as arguing, procrastination, task refusal, swearing, hostile behaviours, hurting others, or the highly motorially restless (under tables and making weird noises, children who wander 'constantly', or who act as if they're a truck on the M1!)

Teachers will face, in any one day, a range of disruptive behaviour — mostly of the 'low-level' but irritating variety as the Elton Report research showed, 1989.

ACCIDENTAL OR PURPOSEFUL?

Children can, will and do 'disrupt' for a variety of reasons. Some may be bored, some children are mischievous (I was); some people like being class clown. Disruptive behaviour may also be related to a child's developmental level; some may not be able to cope with the work, some may be bringing significant socio-emotional baggage from home. If a child comes to school from a 2.00 a.m. flaming row between Mum and Dad (or whoever is masquerading as male care-giver) and has been hauled out of bed by Mum to go to Nan's place, it's hardly any wonder that the child's behaviour may well reflect that at 9.00 a.m. onwards. If Mum is on 'valium sandwiches' to cope with an appalling relationship that sees emotional bastardy visited daily on the child, one hardly has to work at a theory of causation. Schools will need to cater for the welfare of, as well as manage, children from at-risk home environments. Where such situations are identified a whole-school policy is essential (see pp. 99).

STUDENTS' GOALS

Notwithstanding any causative pathology (Rogers 1992b), children also have to 'belong' to their primary social group — the school. Rudolf Dreikurs (1968, 1971) has taught us, what in our saner, more reflective moments we had long suspected, that social behaviour is not accidental but has a purpose — what he called 'mistaken goals': attention-seeking (passive or active); power-seeking (active or passive); revenge (I'll pay you or the system back and force you to notice me!); inadequacy (the child portrays an attitude and behaviour that says I can't belong so I'll withdraw from the social group).

Their behavioural purpose is to send us as quickly as possible up the wall or round the twist — no, only joking (sort of!).

Take **Timothy** in year 4, his teachers say you're quite welcome to! He calls out in class. His teacher says, "Shh! Timmy — how many times have I told you not to call out? Eh?!' He stops for a while, then calls out again. 'Timmy, didn't you hear what I said, how many times do I have to tell you? Put your hand up! Goodness me!!' Here the teacher sighs as if to say 'when will you ever learn?!' Naturally the teacher is annoyed. When Timmy leans back on the chair she often says, 'Do you do that at home?!' 'If you sat up properly you would get more work done', 'Why can't you sit up straight — what's wrong with you?!' He's often caught doing the inappropriate or annoying thing.

As an explanation of social reality Dreikurs argued that students portray a 'goal' behind their behaviour — the students' desire to belong even if it means disruptive behaviour is the *route*.

Timmy gets a lot of attention for doing the wrong thing. When he does put his hand up (without calling out) it is often missed. What does Timothy think of all this?

Lee is Year 7; he comes into class with his baseball cap on. He knows it's against the school rule to wear it in class. Why does he do it? Several of his teachers make it an *issue*:

T   Right, Lee, get it off and give it to me. Idiotic looking hat!

S   No — why should I [Lee puts his hand on his cap. Other teachers have tried to pull it off only to get his acidulated tongue!]

T   I told you, get it off – you know the rule. [Everyone is watching. Lee has an audience. In his 'private logic' he cannot afford to back down. He has to win, but who is calling the shots? Some of his teachers believe they have to win, the 'acronym' can't be allowed to 'get away with it', yet every display of teacher power meets counter power by the student. In this the student's mistaken goal is being met, handed to him on a plate.]

S   Anyway, you can't make me!

T   Yes, I can!!

S   No you can't!

T   You'll be sorry you ever crossed me! [implied teacher revenge.]

The verb 'make' or 'control' means little in this pointless exchange. If the teacher were to remove the struggle (and work privately on the student's attitude) away from the audience, she might have more success. Keeping him back to do lines (he often refuses), ringing his mother (she argues too), sending him to the principal ('Don't care!') only reinforces his mistaken goal. 'I'm important when I force you into a struggle for power where I look like I'm winning.' I've seen students yelled at to leave a class and grin as if to say 'Yeah, well I still won!'

Of course, such student behaviour elicits strong emotion in teachers, the emotion of frustration or anger. That is a powerful clue as to what the student may be after. For example, in a power struggle (trying to get Lee to take off his baseball cap) the emotion teachers often register is anger. This is a clue to what's happening. Surely the student refusing to take off his hat is *not* the cause of our anger? Is it not our desire to control him? Is the child *making* us angry? The ease with which we can play victim ('he made me so angry', 'I can't help my feelings') belies the fact that we can *choose* our responses. Changing our perception by recognising the student's goal is a valuable first step in both avoiding an over-reaction and enabling a more calculated response to disruptive behaviour. Save anger for situations that justifiably merit it.

Chris refused to work in class time. Coming over to him the teacher said, 'You'd better do your work now or you'll be in trouble.' 'Don't care!' 'You will care!' said the teacher. However hard she tried, though, *in front of the rest of the class* the teacher couldn't make Chris do the work.

It could have been dealt with differently if:

- The teacher's attitude was different
- The teacher had recognised the student's goal
- The teacher had some plan (short and longer-term)

T   I notice you haven't started your work.
S   [Student folds his arms, sulkily,] Yeah — well I don't want to do it.

The teacher knows he can do the work. This is task avoidance, a potential power struggle. Aware of his goal she redirects, firmly, but pleasantly.

T   Well Chris, maybe you don't want to do the work but it's the work we are doing today. How can I help you with it?
S   Told you, don't want to — can't make me. [He says this with lowered eyes and sulky voice.]
T   That's right Chris [why not agree — not acquiesce, just agree without sarcasm or rancour] I can't make you, I'm asking you.
S   Don't like this work!
T   Maybe you don't [tune in] but it's the work we're doing today [redirect]. How can I help? [Direct support.]
S   Told you, I don't like it.

At this point the teacher is not going to over-service this minor power struggle. She will leave him to 'own' it within the known classroom rules and consequences.

T   OK Chris, you know our rules; when you need my help let me know.

The teacher then walks off to help someone else, leaving the student to pout, arms folded in 'notice-me' position.

This teacher can work longer term with the student. She can't make him do the work then and there and threats are pointless, they only feed his 'goal'. She can make the consequences (of his 'choice' see p. 90) clear later. For now she gives him take-up time as part of her least to most intrusive discipline. She is balancing correction (in a friendly but assertive way) with respect — leaving the student to experience 'ownership'.

I've seen students use dumb insolence as a form of power exchange. The student hangs his head and refuses to look up, folds his arms and grunts. 'Look at me! — Look at me I said!' The teacher forces the child's head up only to have the child wrench it away, saying nothing but grunting again. Who controls whom? What does the child gain — what is his goal? His goal is power. He is saying 'You can't make me' and he's right.

I worked with a number of first-year teachers at a private girls school a few years ago (a school where students are driven to school in Mercedes and BMWs). A teacher recounted how she had walked up to a Year 10 girl and asked her why she was out of her seat. 'Why?' said the very confident girl, 'I'll give you five reasons why. Reason number one, I was just getting a pencil from my friend. Reason number two, I wasn't disturbing anyone else... [here she ticked off the points on her fingers]. Reason number three, I don't really see it's got anything to do with you Miss. Reason number four, we pay your wages....'

I asked the teacher how she felt during this classroom lawyer exchange. She said she felt both powerless and angry. Before you mentally do a 'Joan of Arc' on this student, consider what she is after. A power struggle. A public argument on these 'points' could be handing the student on a plate the very thing she's after. Whether by pleading or arguing we would give ample wind to her billowing sails. So what do we do? (I'd love to have a student say to me, 'We pay your wages.' I'd put my hand out and say, 'So you're the one, I've been dying to meet you!')

In such situations, what we can do is:

- Recognise the student's goal
- Plan to avoid feeding the goal – be strategic
- Use a balance of short and long-term corrective measures balanced with encouragement

PRIMARY AND SECONDARY BEHAVIOUR

Many students will respond to a teacher's discipline by smart comments, or postural cues, or a tone of voice that is sulky, jaded or hostile by turns.

The teacher addresses the student's *primary* behaviour, the calling out:

T   Cassie, don't call out please.

Quite apart from the 'Don't' (see p. 75). the student immediately launches off into a round of 'secondary behaviours', the extent of which is largely determined by how the teacher responds.

S   Yeah. [Sulky pout] Well, you never answer me, do yer — I had me hand up for ages! [Here Cassie folds her arms in mock (?) sulking.]
T   Well I would answer you if you didn't call out! [Exasperated tone.]

This teacher reply over-services the students *secondary* behaviour.

'Secondary behaviour' is a composite of students' tone, their body language and what they say. The curled lip, the sibilant sigh, the 'tsk tsk' when you ask students to go back to their seat, the tossed head, the closed arms, the way they stand in your spatial presence with just the barest hint of 'compliance', the screwed-up mouth, the raised eyes to the ceiling — these are all very standard postural cues *secondary* to the primary behaviour itself. Students will often add to these cues a tone of voice as if they are the injured party in the social justice stakes. The rising inflection in the voice that says 'Oh!! Come on, all I was doing was talking about the work!' The problem with secondary behaviour is that it often acts like iron filings to a magnet with some teachers. All the teacher sees is a *global* set of behaviour: the tone of voice, the defiant body language and the content of what they say. Some teachers, then, over-service the 'secondary' issues by argument, contest or pleading all of which feed the student's 'goal' of attention or power.

This 'postural cuing' was noted in a Nottinghamshire report, *Black Body Language gets Pupils into Trouble*. It noted that black children are more likely to be excluded from school than whites.

It concluded that black children's body language often leads teachers to think they are arrogant, insolent, defiant, aggressive, disruptive, and 'looking for trouble'. Examples given by teachers included the way Afro-Caribbean pupils look at them, walk in an 'arrogant exaggerated way', display 'dumb insolence', look away when challenged, and suck and hiss their teeth when told off. Intolerance shown by some teachers helped spark conflict. The way Afro-Caribbeans express their particular cultural qualities and the way they walk about school, their facial expressions, their body language, may possibly contribute more to the problem than the fact that their colour is black.

Independent, 11 July 1991

Natalie is in Year 1. In music time the teacher calls the students on to the mat. Natalie stands apart. 'I don't want to! I don't like music. I'm not coming.' She stands well apart, arms folded, head down, a pouting 'don't want to' voice. Rather than getting drawn in, the teacher ignores Natalie (tactical ignoring, see pp. 71-4).

The teacher is aware that if she pleads or forces she might succeed in getting compliance, but at what cost? Finally, Natalie sidles over, sits near the edge of the group as the teacher goes through the song. When Natalie slowly joins in the teacher smiles. When asking for questions, Natalie calls out, but the teacher tactically ignores. Natalie puts her hand up. The teacher smiles, 'Yes, Natalie, thanks for putting up your hand. What's your question?' Natalie says 'It doesn't matter now!' (More secondary sibilants.) The teacher ignores the secondary issue and merely thanks her for putting up her hand and moves on with the lesson.

This teacher has learned not to feed the secondary issues — especially in the public forum. She is aware that students parade 'secondary behaviour' to get their mistaken needs met. She will try to meet those needs by helping the student gain attention, significance and power in *constructive* ways. This is a longer-term process.

Teachers can, of course, create unnecessary secondary behaviour in students by the *way* they address primary behaviour.

James (Year 2) has a toy on his desk in writing time. The teacher walks over, annoyed, and reaches out to grab it.

T   Right, give it to me, now! Come on!
S   I wasn't playing with it! [Sulky look, a clear lying stance.]
T   Don't lie to me!! You were – give it to me!
S   But Richard was playing with his truck before!!
T   I don't care what Richard was doing!

This teacher has 'fed' a whole cycle of unnecessary secondary behaviour.

Rebecca is idly pushing a steel ruler across the workbench in Year 8 woodwork. The teacher walks over and says:

T   Hello Rebecca. What are you doing? [Most students will say, 'Nothing' in answer to this question — not Rebecca.]
S   What's it look like? [The reply is delivered with a curled lip, raised eyes, and a world-weary jadedness, as if to say, 'I'm doing you a favour just being here'].
T   [The teacher does not get drawn in by the secondary 'postural

cues' or by what Rebecca has said. The teacher focuses, for now, on the primary behaviour. 'It looks like you're scraping the ruler across the workbench. What are you supposed to be doing? [This question and feedback is one of several redirection approaches, see p. 84.]

S   Yeah, I know, I know, I'm supposed to be doing my project! [Here Rebecca adds a flounce, eyes to ceiling, and a 'tsk, tsk' for good measure. Again the teacher doesn't argue, to take the 'bait'.]

T   OK. [The teacher actually smiles. Her self-esteem is not bound to Rebecca's approval.] I expect you to go on with your work, if you need my help let me know.

The teacher walks away to help other students. If Rebecca gets on with her work the teacher will come back and encourage as she would any student. In the short term she spends her energy redirecting Rebecca to the primary issue. Later, and longer term, she'll work on Rebecca's attitude — especially after class.

It was an art class, on-task time, Year 9. **Brett** was out of his work spot and noisily time-wasting at another table. While working with one group I 'casually' and expectantly called him over. 'Brett, could you come over here for a minute — thanks.' I resumed my chat as if he'd come. He said, 'What d'yer want?' 'I just want to see you for a minute.' Again I resumed my discussion with the small group. He swaggered over with an exaggerated walk and said loudly, to the 'air', 'Suppose I'm gonna get a detention now!' I ignored that, and when he was over I turned and quietly said 'Can I see you outside for a moment — ta,' and walked to the door as if he'd come. 'What for?!' He came, grumbling. I left the door open, the class carried on.

T   Brett, just a quick word. [I kept a respectful distance, no pointed fingers, no shouting, no big remonstration.] You and I, and the others, have to work in there. I find it difficult to work when you're out of your seat and disturbing others. Also your work doesn't get done.

S   I was only having a chat – Gees!

T   I know you were, [redirection], but I'd like your support on this. Your friends listen to you and it would help. OK?

S   Yeah — no big deal. [Smile.]

Forty seconds it took and we're both back in the room. A private word, just outside the door, helped to keep the attention down, refocus, and enabled a brief repair and rebuild.

Redirecting

T   Brett, you're out of your seat, what are you doing? [Brett is talking to a friend during on-task time in maths.]

S   [Brett picks up his pencil, waves it in the air.] Gettin' a pencil, something wrong with that?

An incipient power struggle. Rather than take the student's postural cues — the chin, the pencil waving, the 'so-what' stance — as a personal traumatic threat, the teacher redirects.

T   You're out of your seat getting a pencil. What should you be doing?

This is said with direct but non-threatening eye contact. The teacher is not throwing down his gauntlet, just refocusing on the important issue *now*. He can address the chip on the shoulder later.

S   Told you [sigh, 'tsk, tsk'], I was getting a pencil.

T   Yes, what are supposed to be doing?

S   In me seat. [Here — what an actor — he raises his eyes to the ceiling and walks back to his own seat.]

The teacher doesn't follow him back, he's already moving off to work with someone else, thus giving Brett some face-saving 'take-up' time. Later the teacher will come back to re-establish a working relationship before the bell goes.

T   OK, I'll come and check your work in a minute. Thanks.

Enough for the moment. What the teacher has done is avoid an *unnecessary* power struggle by accusing Brett of lying, or unnecessary public confrontation, 'Don't you speak to me like that', or 'I don't care what you were doing — I said...!'.

Secondary behaviour: summary

- Make a conscious effort to sort out what is 'primary' and what is 'secondary' behaviour.

- Ask yourself if you're taking secondary behaviour (the sulky tone, the skewed eye contact, the avoidance tactics) as a personal slight, rather than typical acting out of frustration, or an attempt to increase their sense of 'notice-me!', or to make themselves look powerful. Especially resist the effort to 'beat' their last word.

- Plan ahead for when you have to deal with students who display secondary behaviours. Ask yourself if their 'goal' is attention or power. Ask yourself, 'What can I change about my response, my reaction, that will minimise over-servicing of that goal?'

- Recognise that your action as a teacher can affect how much secondary behaviour is displayed by a student. Refusal to buy into a power struggle is an action you can decide. It takes two to argue. While it is appropriate for teachers to get angry on issues that count, when we 'feed' typical secondary behaviour by arguing and taking a win/lose stand we increase the likelihood of secondary behaviour recurring.

- Most secondary behaviour can be *tactically* ignored (see p.71.) It's quiet reading time in Year 3. **Alan** mooches around and won't get a book to sit and join the other quiet readers. This tactic has, in the past, gained him a lot of attention. Rather than getting drawn into a battle with him the teacher reminds him of the quiet reading time rule, 'Alan, it's quiet reading time, I want you to get a book and sit somewhere.' (Alan has a wide choice of reading matter.) Alan puts on a sulky face, drops his head and mutters, 'Don't wanna read, don't like it!' He folds his arms. All these postural cues are tactically ignored by his teacher. She redirects him. 'Maybe you don't want to read now, Alan, but it's SQUIRT time (sustained quiet uninterrupted interesting reading time). I expect you to get a book and settle down.' She says this quietly, but firmly. She walks away as if he will do it. He sulks (more secondary behaviour), she ignores this and walks around the room smiling at the students who are on task. She picks up a book to read herself. Scanning the room she notices Alan slowly get a book and settle. She waits a while and then walks over, smiles, and pats him on the arm. All this briefly (but importantly) encourages him when he's on task. If his behaviour had been loudly disturbing others during the quiet reading time, time-out provision would be used plus longer-term strategies. Time out would normally be prefaced by a 'choice–consequence' approach (see p. 90).

- If secondary behaviour becomes primary behaviour (as when a student hits another on the way back to his seat following teacher direction) the teacher will treat this as a separate incident as she would any hostile aggressive act.

- If secondary behaviour is observed as a 'pattern', deal with it long term on a one-to-one basis (see pp. 91). Short-term strategies are effective when they enable the student to save face, minimise over-attendance and give the student a 'choice' (within fair, class rules).

2

Our Characteristic Style

We all have a **characteristic** management and discipline style, ups and downs and bad days aside. It is seen in the manner, and tone, in which we conduct working relationships with our students, how we speak to them about their behaviour, the tone of our voice, how we present ourselves, whether it comes across that we like or generally dislike our students. Our body language, our bearing, all communicate a message and students are adept at summing up that style: aggressive, sarcastic, hostile, uncaring, indecisive, democratic, wimp....

TWO CONTRASTING STYLES

Mark is a Year 6 student, he is kicking a paper milk carton across the floor in a science lesson.

Teacher A's approach
T What do you think you're doing?! Pick it up! [The teacher has a facial expression of anger, he is pointing to the student, he is tense. This is not acted anger, it's real.]
S It's not my carton, I didn't put it on the floor! [The student's reply is sulky, eyes averted in typical secondary (defensive) behaviour. Did this teacher really expect the student to pick it up, compliantly, no questions asked?]
T I don't care whose it is! What did I say! Idiot!
S [The student continues — he's game!] You *always* pick on me! [He folds his arms in a final, thin, act of insolence.]
T Right, get out, go on, out!

Some of the class are frightened of this teacher, some are angry inside, some (like this student) react in kind. This teacher also resorts to criticism, sarcasm and embarrassment in his desire to win. When children lean back on a chair, he'll pull it back to frighten them or say, 'Don't lean back on the chairs — do you do that at home? Appeals to home 'I don't care if you do that at home; in *my* class...' only inflame resentment — naturally. When students tap pens or rulers he'll snatch or demand they hand them over.

I vividly recall a woodwork teacher once saying to me (Year 10), 'Were you brought up or dragged up, Rogers?!' emphasising his point with a finger jabbed in my shoulder. Incensed (at age fifteen) I said, 'It's none of your bloody business!!', and walked out leaving a shocked and staring teacher. The following week he played the sycophant and I lost the last vestiges of 'respect' I ever had for him.

Whether to an individual student or to a group, hostile, demanding, teachers often don't see their behaviour as necessarily wrong, especially if it achieves its objective — compliance. There are teachers who believe it doesn't matter what you say, or how you say it, and of course it doesn't matter if you *believe* that it will legitimise your actions as a teacher. Such a teacher can achieve 'quiet' and 'obedience', but at a cost to personal dignity and positive working relationships. If you ask him he'll say he's a successful teacher. His beliefs are often couched in demanding terms:

'I *must* win, I can't stand to lose face.'
'Children *must* respect me, *must* do as they are told.'
'Teachers *must* control children. Children *must* be subordinate to their superiors.' (See Rogers 1992b.)

Such beliefs, as an assumptive framework, *create* stress in that when reality doesn't bend or conform, reality is blamed not the degree of demand or the teacher's behaviour. Further, typical secondary behaviour of the student (the sulky voice, the 'disrespectful' body language) is perceived through a cognitive framework of demand rather than preference. To say 'I prefer respect, I enjoy respect' instead of 'Children *must* respect' is different in *kind* as a belief. One is preferential, the other a dogmatic assertion. One can't merely *force* respect through external control — fear yes, respect no. One can desire, invite, model respect and obedience; it is dysfunctional (psychologically stressful) to demand it. The characteristic style of 'aggressive' teachers is marked not by physical force but by:

- Put downs and embarrassment ('Idiot', 'Stupid', 'When will you ever learn?!', 'Are you thick or what?!', 'I'm sick and tired of talking to you, you're *always*...', 'You *never*...!'); sarcasm instead of humour.
- Directly causing the student to lose face.

- Acting on *feelings* of like and dislike rather than working on respect.
- Disenfranchising students' fundamental rights of respect, fair treatment and the right of reply.
- Taking on the responsibilities for the child's behaviour.
- Minimising 'choice' or negotiation.
- 'Telling' rather than directing, arguing rather that redirecting.
- When angry often acting from anger instead of explaining why he or she is angry and allowing cool-off time.
- Imposing rather than negotiating their rules and expectations.

Teacher B's approach

When he sees Mark kicking the carton he sighs and asks nicely, 'Please pick it up Mark.' Mark sulkily argues using his standard line, adding 'Why are you picking on me?!' 'I'm not, Mark, that's really unfair. I don't pick on you. All I asked you to do was...' His voice has a pleading quality, his body language is indecisive, hands outstretched to the side, 'as if' bending to the pressure. The eye contact is uncertain, unstable. If such teachers face criticism they feel rejected, hurt. They tend to avoid conflict by getting caught up in students' secondary dialogue. There is a hesitancy to the voice, a 'softness' easily sidetracked with a lack of clarity about what they really want. This 'style' can be described as non-assertive or indecisive.

If you listen to the pauses, the signs, the tone is often saying in effect, 'Please be fair, like me. What have I done to hurt you, can't you be reasonable?' When pushed this considerate stance sees them shouting or yelling at students and then feeling guilty about their behaviour. In extreme cases such a management style, in teachers, is a recipe for being *seen* as a victim. While we might deplore the way students in a group may act towards such teachers, it is important for teachers to remember that they are classroom *leaders* and their style of leadership sends signals about the *teachers' belief* in their leadership and in the students. Such a style is characterised by:

- A belief that 'I must be liked by my students'. This belief makes it difficult for them to stand up fairly and decisively, for their due rights.
- Children tending to 'walk (all) over them'.
- The rules tending to be unclear or uncertain and infrequently enforced.
- A difficulty in asserting due rights to teach, to fundamental respect.

- Being easily drawn into secondary issues (see pp. 25-9).
- Often a belief that 'This is just the way I am. I can't change, it's just my personality! Nothing I can do can change me.' In its extreme form there is recourse to *personal* explanation of failure.
- When angry, retreating and tending not to explain clearly what it is they are angry about. Also finding it difficult to follow up after an event.

Mark says to his new teacher, when she addresses him about starting his writing, 'I don't like you, you're not as nice as my other teacher.' Some teachers, on hearing this, feel hurt, especially if they believe approval is essential to their well-being and status. 'Mark, that's not nice,' said in an up/down, sing-song voice, 'I work hard for you — I think that's most unfair' This child is not a psychologist but knows how to get 'over-servicing'.

An assertive approach can still be pleasant.

T   You're allowed not to like me [smile], but I'm the teacher who's working with you today. How can I help? [She is firm but pleasant. She doesn't feel guilty or miffed — she doesn't need to. Her self-esteem is not dependent on gaining constant approval.]

ASSERTION

Between the broad extremes of aggressive-demanding and indecisive behaviour is a position that seeks to make one's rights, needs and feelings clear to others without trampling on *others'* rights, needs and feelings. Assertion is to be distinguished from aggression. It doesn't rely on finger wagging, loud voices or testosterone — it is not gender based.

Assertion is a choice we make to be clear, and decisive, as a leader. To be effective assertion needs to be seen as a skill we practise and to be part of a plan. The degree of assertion required to deal with several students calling out will be different from that needed to address sexual harassment.

It is first and foremost a skill

While some teachers are more naturally assertive, most need to learn the skills that can enable teachers to:

- Avoid unnecessary hostility, aggression or indecisive conflict.
- Influence behaviour firmly without shouting, threatening,

pleading, bargaining or fruitless arguing under pressure.
- Legitimise one's emotion without destroying the other person.
- Say 'No', 'I expect...', 'I don't want...', 'I don't like...' with confidence and without feeling guilty.
- Separate primary and secondary issues without getting caught up in guilt at the *need* to assert one's rights or defend the rights of other students.
- Hold reasonable beliefs about teacher–student relationships rather than make absolute demands. Assertive teachers don't demand or plead for approval or praise or respect; they invite, model, expect, work for and often receive respect.

Basic elements of assertiveness

- Be *conscious* of your body language. It signals how relaxed, confident and expectant you are as leader. Practise a relaxed, 'open', posture, facing the person you address. Upright (unless you've got a bad back!) and unapologetic. 'Open' hand gestures rather than pointing at or wagging a finger at. Avoid close, threatening, proximity (see p. 57).
- Direct eye contact is important. When 'up front' it needs to be casually scanning the room and when you need to focus on an individual use direct contact to establish attention. If the student refuses to give it, ask once then speak *as if* they're listening anyway.
- It's not merely what we say that determines how effective communication is, it's *how* we say it. **The tone of our voice**, as well as our general body language and postural cues, convey more than just the words themselves. Try saying the language of discipline (in the following pages) in:
  — a 'fun' or 'light' tone of voice
  — a hostile, aggressive tone of voice
  — a sarcastic tone of voice
  — a pleading, whining, 'be nice to me please' voice
  — an assertive (confident, positive, expectant) tone, as if you expect it to occur

Add to the **tone** a close, overbearing proximity (pointed finger, glaring, tight shoulders); try saying them with an indecisive stance (dropped shoulders, furrowed brows, hesitancy in the voice); try it with a confident, relaxed, upright posture, hand open, outstretched, not too close.

You can see, easily, how important it is to develop congruence between what you say (the content); how you say it (voice tone); and what your body language is communicating.

'But that's my personality — I can't help the way I am.'

If we're in *this* job we'll just have to help it. We'll need to learn to assert (through the tone of our voice, the specific language, and how we follow things through) our rights and needs, as well as protecting others' rights and needs. Letting others 'walk all over us' may be a habit but it is one that can be unlearned.

Of course, personality plays a part. Teachers who generally like children, who have a sense of humour and can actually laugh at themselves and not take every little disturbance as a personal slight, who have a 'presence', who can act a little adding a bit of *joie de vivre* to the lesson, who speak confidently, whose voice is clear and can take on a decisive and assertive tone by turns, who have a natural aptitude for working with people — such teachers have a good foundation on which to build.

Using conscious language repertoire

With practice, and trial and error, I have seen countless teachers become more assertive, more confident and more effective without damaging teacher–student relationships.

A useful strategy is to write down language scripts and practise them. Think of common scenarios and plan a language repertoire. Put it on several cards and do a *daily* practice until it becomes comfortably yours. In the 'emotional moment' you can cognitively script what *you* want to say as classroom leader rather than letting events dictate it for you.

Confidence comes with success. Success is a four steps forward, one step back affair. *Any* success comes with practice, practice within a plan. Get the feel for language, use a tape recorder, even a mirror (stand in front and rehearse!), or a colleague for feedback. Corny as it sounds it can help. After the first few times it gets easier, like most skills.

Conflict/co-operation

- Avoid arguing in a conflict situation. Assert back to the right, rule, fair direction or central issue at stake, speaking in the present tense. Avoid getting drawn into secondary issues (there are many examples in this book of how to do so). If a situation is too tense, defer, or use 'cool-off time'.
- Invite co-operation without forcing it. Demonstrate your

expectation of co-operation by avoiding pointless threats. Use the language of 'choice' instead (see pp. 53-4, 90).

EXPRESSING OUR ANGER

There is a time clearly to express our anger. Significant racism, abuse (verbal or physical or sexual harassment), put downs and teasing merit appropriate anger. The *occasional* 'outburst' to the group is also effective. Where anger is 'weighted', students will get the point. We reduce the currency of anger when we get angry over a host of small incidents.

Anger cannot tell us what to do

Anger is an emotion often arising from frustration at not being able to manage, deal with or control events, circumstances or people. Some people find it easy to lose (or find!) their tempers, especially when dealing with annoying, rude, attention-seeking students. But the emotion *per se* cannot tell us *what* we now need to do.

Managing anger

Even if (and when) our anger is justified, it's worth learning to manage it to our benefit as well as others, rather than giving it free rein or bottling it up.

- What do you normally do when faced with frustrating and anger-creating situations? Do you 'just' react or get hostile? Do you hold back for fear you might go 'over the top'. Do you *communicate* your anger, and the reasons for it? Assertive communication of anger is a skill. Briefly explaining *why* and *what* we're annoyed, frustrated, upset or angry *about* is a skill. Count to three and use 'I' statements, or 'when/then' statements:

  'I don't use language like that with you and I don't expect you...'
  'I get angry when...'
  'I am annoyed because...' (explain then give direction)
  'David, when you call out like that others can't hear. Use our rule, thanks.'
  By explaining why we are angry (even briefly) we avoid giving mixed messages from our seething silences.

'David, when you tap like that I can't teach because...!'

When students (or colleagues) argue, use redirective dialogue, agree *in part* and refocus so the central issue isn't lost. Defer or use cool-off time if their belligerence is not ameliorated by your assertion!

When possible, in class time, direct the student aside to make your point (p. 82). Remember, the degree of assertive anger will be heard as much by your *tone* as by the words. But even high anger can be more effective when directed at the *behaviour* or the *right* being infringed.

There will be times when you are not actually angry but a bit of **acted anger** will carry the point. Use the acted anger to gain attention and then drop the voice to firm assertive level; it communicates the seriousness and the intent.

- Are you aware of the physiological signs of anger in your job? Your tension at natural arousal? Recognising the gritted teeth, the tense shoulders, the bodily constrictions can help. We need to learn to catch ourselves so we can consciously count to three and give ourselves a physiological as well as cognitive advantage.

- When we are overly angry it is appropriate to make a brief point about our anger and withdraw (or have the student withdraw) and allow for cool-off time. There are times when we need time out too! Explain briefly why you're withdrawing from the conflict at this time. Once we start to exchange verbal punches in conflict no one wins. 'Attack the problem, not the person' is very difficult when angry.

- If you do go over the top in an anger episode with students, or colleagues, apologise meaningfully. Explain that you were angry with what they said, or did, not with them personally.

- Keep some perspective on the many frustrations in a teacher's job. A bit of self-humour can help, sharing our experiences, asking others how they cope. It's bottling up that does the damage.

Voluntary/involuntary anger
Maultsby (1977), describing the process of behaviour change, notes

that converting 'practice' means converting one's old *involuntary* emotional habits back to a 'voluntary' state. While we can't stop emotions arising in us (when faced with stressful events), and it's unhealthy to deny them, we can learn to manage them at the point of recognition. This is a skill, a thinking habit, a way of 'choosing' a different perception (Rogers 1992b). I cannot choose my emotion, but I can learn to choose my perception and thus reduce the degree of emotional stress. Such an approach can enable us consciously to address the seeming involuntary competition between 'old' and 'newer' thinking repertoire.

It is not necessary to fall into the trap of saying, 'I can't help it, I *just* get so angry when...'. While rates of frustration and tolerance in teachers vary widely, we can learn to reappraise events so that our reaction is not merely involuntary.

- Imagine yourself faced with a situation that 'creates' frustration in you.
- Try to work out what your beliefs are about it, and what you characteristically say about those events, and then recall your characteristic response.
- Re-imagine the same situation with a new thinking pattern and a different approach.
- Do this from a position of a simple action plan that can enable legitimate, functional, expression of emotion. With the skills discussed in Chapters 3 and 4, reflect on how you went. Fine tune, recognising that it is possible to take some control of the stressful event.
- Discuss scenarios of stressful emotion with your peers to develop professional support in problem-solving and change.

HUMOUR

Humour is a personality trait. Not all teachers (unfortunately) possess a judicious sense of humour. Reparteé, a tasty little *bon mot*, will go down well. Humour can defuse, whereas sarcasm increases defensive emotional arousal. It can even help if we take the joke on ourselves when we misspell, for example, on the blackboard.

One of my colleagues had a student 'send' a paper dart flying towards the blackboard. It fell short — to the giggles of the class. The class wag (*she suspected*) had launched it. She walked over, picked it up, said 'That's what happened to the F1-11s, they never got off the ground either', dropped it in the bin and resumed the lesson to laughter.

You can imagine how it might have turned out had she turned and snapped (or pleaded) 'Right! Who threw that, come on, *who* threw it — it was you wasn't it Jason, come on, it was you?' He would probably deny it and the slanging match is on.

The teacher directed a student who was into heavy chair leaning to put 'four on the floor'. He replied, grinning, 'I have, (two feet, two chair legs). 'OK, go for six! The teacher winked. 'Good one', said the student. 'Wasn't bad was it? Let's see you do it', replied the teacher smiling.

Humour is personality based, of course, but all of us can lighten up a bit. This is the power of defusion — it takes the stress and strain out of a tense moment.

S   This work is real boring. [Leans back grinning as he looks around].

T   This work? Can I have a look? [Teacher smiles as she picks it up, studies it, puts it back and calmly says:] You're right. [Wink. Welcome laughter all round. She adds:] But it's the work we're doing today. If you need my help let me know. [She will re-establish with this student later.]

I walked into an English class recently and a student said, 'What shit are we doing today?' Complete with a Megadeath tee-shirt, he turned to his peers to 'preen'. I walked over, and in a loud whisper (the class was quiet) said, 'The interesting kind', and winked. Later I was able to involve him in the lesson and actually had him 'on-side'. I found out he was a 'poor reader' and often used clowning to gain some group prestige.

S   [First day] Are you married Miss? [Wink, raised eyes]

T   What is this, a proposition Steven?

S   [In biology] If there's not enough food we could eat people! [Class clown starts snorting]

T   OK Steven, we'll start with you.

S   [Year 11 boy to a new (and attractive) female teacher, in front of the class:] Wanna date? [Snort, snort]

T   Keep dreaming, Jason. [She says this with a wink.]

Sarcasm does the opposite, it increases the 'heat' and the resentment; and if I can be allowed an Australianism, it 'boomerangs'. Sarcasm comes across in tone, in attack language, in intentionally making the student look foolish.

ENCOURAGEMENT

The key to encouragement is the building of courage (Dreikurs 1968): courage to try, courage to fail, courage to be, courage to keep trying.

It's strange but children actually improve with encouragement in that *this* teacher, *this* parent, *this* care-giver believes in you and your effort even when failure is part of the journey. It helps children to want to go on with their effort if they feel, and believe, that their teacher sees the successful *effort*. Even failure can be taught to be seen as constructive for growth.

Like other aspects of management, it's *how* we encourage as well as what we say: our tone, the tactile address; the expectation we convey; the body language (smile, wink, thumbs up, the OK sign, pat on the shoulder with the 'well done').

'Hey, that's good thinking Jason.' (with respect to Jason's idea)
'OK, it's hard but you'll get it if you hang in there. I know you'll do it.' (confidence)
'I knew you could do it!' (accomplishment)
'I appreciate it when...'
'I like the way you did that...'
'OK, you made a mistake, what can we learn from it — or how can we fix things?'

It's OK to make mistakes — even fail. Failure doesn't make one a failure. Self-talk that says, 'I *made* a mistake, OK, what can I learn from it?' or 'OK, I made a mistake, I'm fallible, how can I fix things?' is better all round than 'I am a failure'. No one can *be* a failure (unless they believe it and re-indoctrinate themselves by psychological junk mail — Rogers 1992b).

An encouraging environment
Adults can and should work at creating an environment for children where they can know they are secure:

- They can fail without being laughed at or put down
- They can learn through their failures as well as their successes
- They can be accepted as part of the group.

Even just the way we start the day with our children. If they hear us moaning and complaining every day, hear us picking on all their habits, nagging them to pick this up, do that, what kind of effect is it likely to have?

Each day we can consciously try to make our children's day a little bit more positive by *thinking about what we say*. Look out for the small positive things they do and trying to encourage them in those things.

Ask yourself how you like to be spoken to, encouraged, supported and try to relate to the children that way. It's basic *respect*. We can't expect teachers to like all their children — we often cannot help our feelings about children we don't naturally like but we can respect them. Treat them fairly, support them, encourage them. Respect is something you can *do*. It doesn't simply depend on feelings.

The language of encouragement

Ill-considered: 'Don't leave the lids off those paints they'll...'
Considered: 'Put the lids back on, then they won't dry out.'

Ill-considered: 'Don't use the brush unless you've washed it. How many times have I told you, eh?!'
Considered: 'Use the brush after you've washed it, thanks.'

Ill-considered: 'If you hold it like that it's no wonder you can't paint properly.'
Considered: 'What's a comfortable way to hold the brush? OK. I want you to try holding it like this, a bit like holding a pencil, isn't it. Let's practise.'
Ill-considered: 'Don't...'
Considered: 'Do...'

When you see the student doing the appropriate actions, remind by encouragement. 'Well done David, you remembered to wash your brush before you used the other colour.' 'Thanks for remembering to put the paint lids on. They won't dry out now will they?' (Wink). 'Thanks for remembering to put your chair under.' (Smile)

Unnecessary negative tone without a balance of encouragement just breeds resentment or an attitude that 'gives up'.

Practice

Sometimes children (of any age) fail because they're not clear about the required action. Practice can help. This is especially important when developing behaviour-plans with students on a one-to-one basis (see pp. 101-2).

'Here, let me show you.'
'Now, you practise.'
'Now, how do you think you did?' (Self-evaluation)

Responding to positive behaviours

It is easier to notice and respond to negative behaviour. While it is necessary to address negative and disruptive behaviours, it is also necessary to balance correction with encouragement. A language of encouragement is essential to balance a language of discipline:

- Be conscious about the need to encourage.
- Be specific in your encouragement by addressing the effort or improvement. 'David, I appreciated the way you joined in class discussion today.'
- Older students will prefer more 'private' than public praise. Take them 'aside' in class to encourage.
- Even the pedestrian smile, 'Thanks for...', 'I'm pleased you remembered', 'It helps when you... thanks' have an effect. 'Global' praise is far less effective, i.e. 'good' boy 'good' girl or 'good' thing. Rather 'You're pleased with that piece of writing, aren't you?' It can be phrased as a question, 'How do you think you did?' Ask students to evaluate their own behaviour compared to past performance. Make it a habit. It can be worth while to record something positive you notice (co-operation, packing up, neat desk, improvement in an area of work or behaviour) and give the encouragement later when you've got time. It's easy to forget.
- Positive notes can help (relating to work or behaviour) and a call to parents now and then can work wonders.
- With academic work use descriptive assessment approaches. Avoid the big 'wrong' marks and red lines. Unobtrusive marking will especially help struggling writers. Correct spelling in the margin, or attach daily spelling lists, rather than having heavy crossing outs blotching the page.
- As I like to draw I append cartoons to students' work with talk bubbles giving the specific phrase. Stickers, stamps, notes (in the diary) of a positive nature can all lift the game.
- Merit awards in class, for other than academic work, can boost morale and a sense of achievement.
- Avoid taking away 'rewards' earned (especially in those schools using points tallies) or adding disclaimers or qualifiers to your encouragement. It devalues it.

For the *whole class* there can be reinforcers such as:

- Free activities, morning or afternoon tea.
- In one very difficult Year 6 we tied on-task time and positive social behaviour to a points chart. When the class reached 100 points, the reward was board games; 200 meant afternoon tea; 300 a barbeque. It was one of the things that significantly improved the tone of the class as well as its social behaviour.
- Outside classes on the lawn.
- Class music listening (volume selected by the teacher and veto on heavy metal!).
- Merit-awards or tokens are given for display of positive social attitudes. These can be shown to parents and after a set number a pen, book, school mug, free lunch vouchers or place mat can be given.

Like most visible and more 'public' awards, their use needs monitoring. A whole-school approach setting out the kind of rewards and how they are administered will be effective.

It is important that realistic standards, and opportunities, be set for positive behaviour and the application be genuine. This will come across, as most things do, in our manner — using their first name, our body language, the light pat on shoulder or back, the wink, the smile, an open and approachable manner.

Checklist on encouragement

- Are you aware of how you encourage positive behaviours in students, especially the more annoying ones you don't easily like?
- How specific is your praise and encouragement?
- How can you help students to appreciate their *effort* in work, in behaviour? How can you help them to contribute to *this* class?
- How can you enable students to see how far they have come in work and in behaviour?
- Do you keep a 'list' (a notebook) of areas where you can give feedback to students over and above your formal assessment?
- How descriptive is your assessment? What concentration do you make on the 'wrongness' of their work and the effort and potential in their work? Descriptive assessment (based on the student's ability and goals) is not as easy as red marks and ticks and crosses (or a 'good work') but it is more likely to focus on strengths and encourage effort.

Self-image and self-esteem

John Powell (1976) has said, 'A good self-image is the most valuable psychological possession of a human being.' Our daily interaction with our students can enhance a stronger self-image just as the sum of the interactions in our lives assists in our own self-image. Of course, at the end of the day self-esteem is just that: *self*-esteem, the value we place on ourselves *as a self*, but small children and many adolescents build (and believe) their self-esteem from *other* esteem; this is the power a teacher has. Many students at secondary level will say in one year how much they hate maths and in the following year how 'great' maths is. The difference? Their self-image in relation to maths has changed. The key variable? The teacher and how he or she is working with that student. Where self-esteem is high children *feel* they can do better, they then come to *believe* they can do better. Their sense of social identity is strengthened (I am cared for as a person); their sense of competence is strengthened (I can do this); and their sense of security is enhanced (I feel safe here — emotionally safe) (Coopersmith 1967). The *balance* between correction, encouragement and pastoral care will enhance self-esteem but like everything else in this job we'll need to 'plan' for it and build it into our teaching repertoire.

CASE STUDY 1: YEAR 2

Ms Dennis is a Year 2 teacher, twenty-five students; the school is considered a 'hard' school. Some of the boys can be extreme in their attention-seeking, and she has a couple of 'testing' girls. The five 'harder' students all have some compounding home problem.

Ms Dennis's attitude is, while I can't do much (sometimes nothing) about their home environment, there's a lot I can do when they come into 'my' classroom and our school. She is not afraid to seek peer support when needed but has built her classroom discipline and management on a planned approach utilising fundamental protocols (p.153) and skills that answer the four questions:

- How can I **prevent** unnecessary disruptive behaviour?
- How can I **correct** disruptive behaviour when it occurs.
- What **consequences** can I apply where correction doesn't work?
- How can I **repair and rebuild** after I've disciplined and applied consequences?

These are planning questions that shape her discipline and management plan.

1. In what way can I prevent unnecessary disruption by planning ahead?
She has published the clear, fair, rules on large cards with pictorial cues (p.112). She discussed this thoroughly week one, day one. She refers back to '*our* fair class rules' day after day by reminders, encouragement, questions. She has also prevented *unnecessary* disruption by having well-thought out routines for entering and leaving the class; coming on to the mat at the beginning and end of the lesson; showing work to the class; monitor systems (so all get a chance); equipment usage; clean-up routines (she has simple games to encourage and make it fun). She has reminder posters with pictures for key routines such as clean-up, use of the wet area, lunch-time, what to do if you have a problem. She also has a number of 'in-reserve' games, songs and short stories for on-the-mat time. She also uses these for distraction and diversion activities.

At the beginning of the day she has the 'jobs' (work tasks) for that day listed with a little cartoon for the less able readers. She has several 'activity areas' (often changed daily) where children can work at their own pace beyond the 'set work'. She has organised her groups by mixed ability and *teaches,* and then encourages, co-operation in her students. She has set aside time in her programme to *teach* listening skills (with eye contact, checking to see if the other person has heard, and student-to-student encouragement). She uses a number of simple games to enhance self-esteem.

She has asked herself a lot of questions in advance as part of preventative management:

- Can the children move comfortably around the room?
- Have I made the routines for... clear? Have I established fair, clear workable rules? Have I made class consequences fair?
- Have I checked if they know and understand what to do when...?
- How can I rotate monitors? What jobs can I entrust monitors with?
- What is a good routine for going to the toilet in Reception and Years 1 and 2?
- How can I keep noise level workable at on-task time, quiet for mat time and silent for silent reading time?

All these questions may seem basic but that's the whole point — answer the basics and you're well on the way to positive prevention.

2. How can I correct (in such a way as to balance assertion and respect, and self-esteem)?
If you watch Ms Dennis correcting you will see (and hear) firmness and expectation but never malice or a simple equating of the child with his behaviour.

- 'Hands up Sean, without calling out thanks'. She says it briefly, positively, with expectation and quietly 'picks up' those *with* their hands up.
- 'Remember our walking rule (smile), thanks Sean'. He walks.
- Paul, what do you need to remember before you go to the painting table? (Rather than 'Don't forget to...' or 'No, you're not going to the painting table until...'.)
- 'Oliver,' (wink) 'Show me four on the floor.' (This is a reminder to stop chair leaning.) If Oliver (or any student) shows a high frequency of chair-leaning, or calling out, or seat-wandering, or butting in, or teasing, she will make a special one-to-one plan as well as use class-based consequences (see p. 120).
- 'I'm pleased with the way you're sitting still and listening, Craig.' This is said briefly, with a smile, to one of the very restless. She uses lots of encouragement like this hour after hour. 'You're proud of what you're doing, aren't you Craig? Would you like to show the class later?'
- She has a wide range of privately understood signals (see p. 74) to convey intent and expected behaviour. Fingers to lips rather than 'shush, shush'. Hands up to indicate when it's required, hands in laps (modelled) with a wink to convey attention when on the mat. If you watch her, *all* these multiple behaviours, with the steady and pleasant tone, seem to merge into an easy whole pattern. She calls the group to the mat with one of her many games, a counting game: 'I'm counting to 30 and I want you all on the mat. Let's go, 1, 2...'
- 'OK, all those with green eyes on the mat! All those with blue skirts (or lace-up shoes, or beautiful freckles, or brilliant language skills — that's all of you!!), all those with one brother, a white cat...'

In effect she works at relationship-building by balancing greetings (in and out of class), encouragement, remembering little things about the child and their family as well as special events like birthdays, etc (using birthday charts, colourfully illustrated).

Several students want to show their work, a project on prehistoric animals. Sean, Chris and Eleanor. As they get their work the teacher reminds them of the 'excuse me' rule (part of the manners rule): 'Sean, Chris and Eleanor, before you come up to the front past all the other seated students what do you need to remember?' They don't appear to know, then Eleanor cottons on, 'Oh, scuse me!' Ms Dennis smiles, 'OK, go for it.' They say 'Excuse me' to the other children (reinforcement of the manners rule) and the 'Red Sea' parts. When they are up at the front she says, 'How can you hold the work so that everyone can see?' (Rather than, 'Don't hold it like that, no one will be able to see it down there, will they?!') She is aware that her daily language can build in *corrective language* with encouragement. 'That's it, Sean, under your chin.' 'Are they all looking? That's right, Sean, check their eyes.' Here she thanks a couple of students (the fidgeters) for sitting and looking. As Sean explains his work, she asks several open questions and invites audience feedback. Her 'style' is not mere personality. She has worked at her craft especially the language of correction and encouragement.

Many children come to school without manners. Ms Dennis, by encouragement and reminder and games, teaches 'please', 'thanks', 'ta', 'may I borrow', put things back as (and where) you found them, take care, watch people's space, 'excuse me', apologise if you accidentally bump, share and co-operate. She discusses manners through stories, situations and rule reminder and encouragement when good manners are practised.

If any children come in from playtime with a problem (including tears), rather than stop the whole lesson and try to run a mini court case she uses the class problem-fixing rule (see p. 115).

Looking directly at Eleanor who (crying) says, 'Miss, Rebecca isn't my friend no more she's going wiv Katie and do you know they said, they said....' Ms Dennis gently butts in. 'Eleanor, I can see you're upset (tunes in and lets her know she understands) but we're starting class now. Take a tissue (or she might ask another student to get a tissue — an essential aid — helps the sniffles) and sit over here' (pleasant but appropriately firm.) Katie says, 'It's a lie Miss...!!' 'Katie,' Ms Dennis beckons to the other side of the floor space, 'Away from Eleanor, I can see you're upset. I want you to sit here.' She will not brook discussion now while they're upset. (If there is blood she'll send them to the first-aid teacher under escort!)

Later when they've cooled right down she will offer a problem-fixing time. She has a corner where they can do this. The poster has cartoons with three questions:

- What happened?
- Why?
- What can we do to fix things?

Where possible Ms Dennis encourages the children to fix things themselves. She taught this process in the first week and often goes over to the 'corner' to help them start. More serious conflicts are settled after class with the teacher as third party mediator. Some problems (affecting more than a few) may require a classroom meeting (see p.133f).

Number one rule, though, is we can't solve problems when we are upset or angry. We have to have cool-off time first.

In her corrective discipline she balances *tactical* ignoring (where and when appropriate) with a wide repertoire of least to most intrusive correction (see Chapter 1). She has a language of discipline. Even when she gets angry (she gets angry, mostly, on issues that count — put downs, sexist behaviour, racist behaviour, hurting), she seeks to separate anger *about* from anger *towards* 'I get angry when...', 'I am angry because...' is said with emotion and effect. If she feels she's gone over the top she apologises.

Consequences

In applying consequences she tries to telegraph, in advance, the if–then consequences for breaches of safety, unfair treatment of other students, or significant upsetting of other students' learning.

Some consequences have to be deferred to 'after' class — even then she asks them to 'own' it by saying:

- What did you do?
- What is our rule?
- What can you do to fix it?
- How can I help you?

Repair and rebuild

When applying consequences she also works on repairing and rebuilding the relationship. She avoids holding grudges; she starts each day afresh.

She has an impressive array of skills, she has *learned* most of them. She has a hard job. She's a teacher.

CASE STUDY 2: YEAR 8

Mr Smith walks towards his 8D, he gets there on time. Basic, but it helps. Maths class, period five. He's tired, it's a full day (every timetable slot). They're a testing class, he had some of them in Year 7.

Class rules
He has a positive approach, having established class agreements *with them* on the way they 'will' treat one another; how they'll communicate, learn, move in, move out, and move around the room (including toilet routines); how they'll settle any disputes (individuals and as a class). In science he also has specific safety rules. General safety in maths has been discussed under the treatment/manners agreement. He has emphasised rules under the rubric of rights and responsibilities.

Routines
He has also established basic class routines for distribution and retrieval of materials (especially in science), work requirements, how to get his assistance as teacher (he's taught them the rule 'check with three before you check with me'). He has also worked on noise level using the novelty approach of a noise-meter (see p.126). Some of the students recall it from Year 7. 'Noise monitors' keep an eye on the noise-meter during class work-time. He also has a monitor system (rotated) for a number of basic jobs freeing him to teach (this is important in teaching subjects such as art, music, textiles, materials design technology, etc.).

Normality of disruption
However well and interestingly he plans his units of work, and individual lessons, he is realistic enough to know there is a normality to many disruptions: calling out, butting in, clowning, talking out of turn, seat-wandering, task avoidance, and so on. He plans for these, conscious that what he says (characteristically), when disciplining, will set the tone of the room.

Beginning the lesson
The topic is number lines (positive and negative integers). Mr Smith draws a straight railway track on the board as the children file in. Turning he waits (scanning the room) and notices several students settling down. He calls them by name, 'Daniel, Melissa, Wayne, Paul,

thanks for settling down.' He doesn't over-attend to the noisy ones. He then pauses, quickly draws a train on the tracks, and gives a general direction in a louder voice. 'OK, everyone facing this way please' or 'Right! Let's do the three routine. OK? Sit up, settle down, face this way' (wink and smile) or 'I need you facing this way and listening please.' He pauses, waits for natural settling time (a 'privately understood signal'.).

He says, 'Good morning' (greetings are basic courtesy) and recaps. Jason butts in, 'Ay you didn't draw no wheels on the train' (snort, snort!!). He looks, laughs, 'Look at that — no wheels — how is that train going to positivise and negativise the numbers, eh? Thanks Jason. Come on (he gives Jason some attention) artistic assistance please.' This is a distraction and diversion. He pats Jason on the shoulder as he grins his way back to his seat. As the lesson proceeds there is some calling out and talking out of turn. Several students call out, he tactically ignores them and gives a general rule reminder (p.80) 'Remember our rule, everyone, for questions.' 'Yes, Michelle.' He signals Michelle who has her hand up. 'Thanks — what's your question?' He uses his hands (raising his right hand) as a confirmatory 'signal'. He also 'blocks' with his other hand those who butt in. Sometimes he adds a brief reminder, 'Sam, one at a time, thank you.' His 'up-front' discipline is brief, positive, expectant, and always prefaced by first names. He works hard at remembering and using first names in and out of class. If he's not sure he checks but also uses seat plans and looks at diaries as he moves around the room. Sometimes he'll quietly ask one student another student's name prior to moving over to address that student. He's aware of the social dimension of the teacher–student relationship.

Two students are talking while he explains the 'addition' of positive and negative numbers on the railway track example. 'Melissa and Donna, I want you to face this way and listen, thanks.' He uses 'I' statements and directions frequently. As he refocuses on the lesson (by moving his eyes away, back to the board and the class) Melissa has to have the sulky 'last word'. 'We're only talking about the work.' Mr Smith doesn't argue or discuss, he briefly (almost casually) redirects. 'Agreeing' in part he says, 'I'm sure you were but I want you to face this way and listen, thank you.' As he resumes the lesson Melissa sighs, folds her arms and 'complies'.

Daniel is in heavy and noisy chair-lean mode. 'Daniel,' (he establishes eye contact) 'Feet down thanks,' (wink) 'Four on the floor and facing this way, thank you.' As he resumes the lesson, Daniel sighs, eyes to the ceiling, and noisily rights the chair. Mr Smith keeps the flow of the lesson going. When Daniel *is* attending he smiles in his direction. He tactically ignores 'low-level' disruptions where possible but where a disruption affects his right to teach or another student's right to learn or be treated with respect, he'll 'discipline' by non-verbal signals, reminders, directions, questions or distractions. In Mr Smith's mind is a 'plan'; a repertoire of least to most intrusive possibilities. He'll juggle these according to context.

Whenever he uses directional language 'up front' he tries to focus on the behaviour expected and avoids 'giving' mixed messages ('How many times do I have to!!!' 'What's wrong with you?!). Daniel clicks his fingers to gain attention. Mr Smith tactically ignores Daniel. Daniel sighs, leans back a bit, keeps clicking. Pauses and wearily puts his hand up. 'Yes Daniel, what's your question?' 'Doesn't matter now!' Daniel folds his arms and pouts. 'Well thanks for putting your hand up.' He carries on with the lesson, not responding to Daniel's obvious 'baiting'. Paula asks a question about the use of subtraction on the number line, getting muddled. A few laugh. The teacher says 'Good one, Paula, for having a go! You're right about going backwards on the line'. All these disruptions are dealt with in a brief in/out way, never over-dwelling on any one incident. Anyone watching would see a relaxed 'flow' to both the teaching and brief discipline (a 'flow' that belies the conscious repertoire — his *aide-mémoire*).

On-task time
Mr Smith directs the students to their class activity. Later in the year he'll use a mix of small group work (including co-operative learning) and whole-group teaching and learning.

Michael comes up whining, 'I haven't got a pen!' Michael utilises whines and task avoidance to gain over-servicing from his teachers. 'That's all right, Michael, borrow one of mine — just hand over your guarantee.' 'What?' 'Your watch, gym shoes, comic?' Mr Smith hasn't lost any of his class pens, rulers or compasses. (An alternative is to have some class pens, pencils, rulers with yellow tape around and room number noted!)

During on-task time Mr Smith walks around the room reminding, checking, encouraging. It's also easier to give more ' private' discipline this way.

If there's any eating, or comics, or 'toys', he'll give a brief, simple, choice. 'Anna, I want you to put that deep and meaningful comic in your bag or on my desk' (wink). This least intrusive approach is generally enough. If the students procrastinate he redirects (with humour on his 'good' days). He also uses least intrusive measures when students are abstractedly off task. Tom is staring out of the window. 'How's it going, Tom?' This casual question draws Tom back on task without a big fuss. He sometimes uses *direct* questions in the same way. 'What are you doing Tom?' He is aware that the *tone* of his voice can easily change the meaning and intent of *what* he says when managing and disciplining.

Re-establishing working relationships

If he disciplines any student he will make the effort to go back to them before the bell, or briefly after class, and re-establish the teacher–student relationship. When they are back 'working' he'll often just walk by and say, 'How's it going then?' 'Thanks for settling into it, can I see your work, please?' If any student refuses to show him the work he'll repeat (once) and then leave them with the conditional 'When you're ready, let me know.' He doesn't over-service their attention-seeking (in the short term) but will follow up on this at a later stage.

Melissa is out of her seat bending down in heavy-weather discussions with Lisa. Mr Smith walks over and directs her back to her seat. 'Oh! I was only getting a pencil from Lisa' (hands on hips). He tactically ignores her 'notice-me' stance (see p. 71) and redirects, 'Maybe you were but I want you to go back and work at your own desk, thanks.' He is sure she is lying but doesn't cause her to 'lose face' publicly. He walks away (giving her 'take-up time'), still casually scanning the room. In less than half a minute she 'sidles' off to her desk. When she's working he goes over to check her work.

David isn't doing his work. Mr Smith comes over. 'David, I notice you haven't started. What's the problem?' 'Don't like this work, it's boring.' 'You're right, David, not all our work is interesting. How can I help?' He distracts him to the easier part of the lesson, the train diagram. David struggles with maths but Mr Smith has a supportive attitude, jockeying him along with some specific goal-directed work to cater for his ability level. If students refuse to do the work he knows he can't make them but he makes the consequence clear by way of a 'choice' (see p. 90).

Daniel is noisily chatting to Chris. Mr Smith is trying to help David, the noise is too high, he 'splits attention' by briefly directing across three desks, 'Chris, noise down, thanks, I'm working here with David and Michael.' Towards the end of the lesson he hears Chris call David 'an idiot'. It wasn't too loud but loud enough. Mr Smith beckons him over. 'Chris, I want to see you over here for a minute.' Chris mooches over. He beckons him to the side of the room. 'Chris, when you say 'idiot' that's a put down. Put downs hurt.' 'I was only joking!' 'Maybe you were but we've got a class rule for respect. Use it, thank you.' Chris goes back. The tribal tom-toms will get the message. If the original 'offence' had been louder the rule-reminder would have been more public, more assertive.

The close of the lesson
As the lesson draws to a close he uses a group reminder. 'OK, folks, remember to put your chairs under the tables, thanks, and any litter by your feet in the bin, thanks.' 'James,' Mr Smith beckons to some paper near him. 'S'not mine!' 'I'm sure it's not, James, but in the bin mate, thanks.' James grumbles, sighs and 'tsk, tsks' as he showily puts it in the bin. 'Thanks James,' he ignores the 'postural cueing'. He also uses privately understood messages like 'OK' signs, thumbs-up signs (to indicate well done), a frown or smile or hand block. These simple indicators of encouragement and discipline save words but still convey intent.

LESSONS TO BE LEARNED

Both these teachers are using a skilled approach to discipline, balancing the corrective and supportive.

- The positive outcomes are not accidental, they are planned as part of their total teaching responsibility. They do not see discipline as an end in itself but a purposeful means to the end of balancing rights, responsibilities and accountability.
- They avoid over-servicing attention-seeking and getting drawn into power struggles. Using assertive skills they have learned to balance their needs and rights without intentionally damaging students' rights and needs.
- Being fallible they don't always get it right but a plan helps keep the primary issues in focus. On the days they get it wrong they're forgiving of themselves and the students. In this (they're not unabashed about apologising) they build the workable relationships that are the heart of effective discipline and management.

3

Making a Discipline Plan

BUILDING A SKILL REPERTOIRE: LEAST TO MOST INTRUSIVE

A discipline plan is essentially a conscious awareness of what one can, ought, and will seek to do and say in discipline transactions. This plan has at its heart an acute awareness of how essential language, and language *use*, is, as a tool to service discipline transactions. 'Scripted' repertoire is set out with the assumption that developing a balance between appropriate assertion and dignity and respect is actually a skill. A range of scripts for 'discipline language' is set out later in the text.

There are many elements running together when we address disruptive behaviour:

- Tone of voice
- Eye contact
- Proximity and general body language
- Context and 'matching'
- Brevity and 'take-up time'
- Re-establishing working relationships, balancing 'short' and 'longer' issues

Juggling these elements *together* so they flow requires practice — conscious practice. If you watch an effective teacher the elements above take on a *characteristic whole*.

Tone of voice
Does our tone convey expectation, hostility, sarcasm, incipient or over put down, indecisiveness or assertion? Tone of voice puts a significant *weighting* on the words we use.

Eye contact
It is normal in Western culture to see eye contact as an attention-

gaining cue; it establishes attention and rapport. Of course, if eye contact becomes a stare (especially in an 'up-front' classroom setting) it may convey threat and potential power struggle. After a few seconds of eye contact look away or add a verbal direction to convey why you want *their* attention and response. If (as in some cultures) eye contact is not established, it is unwise to force it (hand under chin, 'Look at me!'). Speak to the ears if not to the eyes. On a one-to-one basis (later) it can be explained to the student why eye contact is preferred and appreciated.

Proximity

Being too close, overbearing (sitting on a student's desk) may telegraph threat and implied force. For example, there are teachers who walk up to students and just take their work off the desk to comment (or mark it). They may tap the exercise book and make judgements such as 'What kind of work do you call this?' 'Is this all you've done?' Basic respect can be demonstrated by coming into personal space in an invitational manner. 'Can I see your work, please?' 'Where are you up to (in your work)?' 'How's it going, Sean?' I had a student, recently, who looked surprised when I asked him if he minded me writing a correct spelling in his margin. He wasn't used to it. I believe *even* asking if you can look at their exercise book (or whatever) shows fundamental respect.

General body language

Pointing at students; or waving the poking, threatening finger in the air near them; poking their work or hand slamming the desks; sitting on their desks (without asking); crowding them — these are all acts that indicate overt power by spatial presence. Use of an open hand when making a point is far less intrusive then gesticulating, pointing fingers.

Body language can also signal indecision and non-assertion. Slumped shoulders, darting unstable eye contact, hands palm upwards, leaning forward head down, coupled with sighs and a pleading tone may signal 'this teacher is a bit of a walk-over'. When children are in a group they pick up these 'signals' quickly.

Context

The context determines the kind of discipline we use. In each 'lesson' there is an establishing phase as the class troops in, settles to their seats, table (or position in physical education or drama). Then the teacher has to gain the attention of the group and focus it on the lesson or activity. This 'up-front' phase requires brief discipline that avoids over-dwelling. It would be inappropriate, for example, to walk from 'the front' across to the two or three chatterers and confront them. 'Why are you three talking!' or 'Don't talk when I'm teaching!' This only serves to over-service any attention-seeking already existing. The directions or reminders can be delivered from a confident leadership position 'up front'. Speak 'across' the room in a clear voice, 'David, Daniel and Kelvin, (pause here to establish attention) facing this way and listening, thank you.' If they answer back we can briefly redirect (see later, pp. 87-9). Eye contact is decisive, but after the across-the-room direction has been given the teacher immediately resumes the lesson *as if* the students will respond. When up front it's normally more effective to use general directions (when there's noise from several students) or individual directions or reminders. During 'on-task' time the discipline can be more personal, one to one. Attention during 'on-task' time is divided between task and appropriate working noise, so the teacher can move around the room on a more interactive one-to-one basis.

Matching

It is also important to match the discipline approach to the degree of, and nature of, the disruption. It is inappropriate to make a big scene over, say, chewing gum or uniform misdemeanours. For 'chewing' a more privately understood signal may be enough (motion to mouth, wink, and point to the bin) or a brief rule reminder. 'Dave, you know the rule for chewing gum — in the bin, thank you.'

Essentially 'matching' refers to relating the *degree* of intervention to the degree to which the disruptive behaviour affects the teacher's right to teach and students' rights to learn and feel safe. When David put a female student down, in one of my classes, I called him aside and (quite annoyed) said, 'David! That's a put down and put downs hurt'. He replied, 'Was just mucking around!' 'Maybe you were but we've got a rule for respect, I expect you to use it.' Later I re-establish with David (when the heat had gone down) and an apology was offered to the other student. There are appropriate issues on which to get angry (racist, put-down behaviour). Directions, reminders, casual questions, would precede in-class consequences on a least to most intrusive basis.

Back to low-level disruption like eating in class. Melissa has a packet of chewing gum on her desk and is chewing it in class. The real issue (at that point in the short term) is not the social justice of eating in class, but that it's the rule (a rule that helps the cleaner and carpet alike!). It is wiser not to address a gum-chewer in the public up-front sense; wait until on-task time. Chewing gum does not affect the instructional delivery.

T   Melissa, chewing gum in the bin, thanks. ['Thanks' conveys expectation.]

S   It's only chewing gum, c'mon! [Sigh, folded arms, eyes to ceiling to exacerbate the social justice intrusion.]

T   That's right, it's only chewing gum [teacher doesn't take all these postural cues as 'bait'] but it's a school rule. In the bin, thanks.

S   All right! [Here Melissa sighs and goes over to spit it (*dramatis personae*) into the bin. All well and good. I've had many students, though, who extend the teacher direction unto the 'last-word syndrome'.]

Here the teacher walks away as if the student will comply. The walking away also signals appropriate public 'face-saving' to the student; it also allows student take-up time and emotional withdrawal.

The teacher moves off to work with other students as Melissa mutters off to the bin a minute or so later (in 'her' time). Who won? It's not a matter of winning but of leading the student in such a way as both 'win' and the student owns the behaviour. If the student refuses to put the chewing gum in the bin (it's only a minor issue) the teacher can give a quiet consequence reminder. The teacher beckons Melissa over and says, 'Melissa, I've asked you twice (asked not told) to put the gum in the bin. You know the rule. If you choose not to you're choosing to see me at break.' 'C'mon, it's only chewing gum!' 'True, but it's a school rule Melissa.'

Melissa wanders off and puts it in the bin. If she doesn't the teacher can let it go at that point in the lesson, leaving the ball in the student's court as it were (the teacher can't *make* her put the chewing gum in the bin) and follows up later. After all, it is the *certainty* of the follow up that is important. At no time has the teacher allowed a minor disruption to take on combative proportions.

Brevity

The longer we gas on and nag the more convoluted and heated the discipline becomes. Students tend to go deaf after the first few sentences especially if the teacher's tone is perceived as 'soap-boxish'. If we get caught in long discussions, debates and arguments (when the audience of peers is watching) we feed attention-seeking and power-seeking in the student.

Brief directions, reminders, questions, choices and redirections are more effective when the transaction is affected by emotional arousal. 'David', (use first names) 'I want you to put your hand up without calling out' — this can be said with a smile, a wink or a frown. It can be said with a fun tone or a more assertive tone (depending on the degree of intrusiveness to rights). Calling out can even be tactically ignored. We have to use professional judgement based on our plan and knowledge of the students (where possible).

The longer we make the direction, reminders, question, the more difficult it is to get the essential point over. We may also end up giving mixed messages, 'I'm sick and tired of...', 'How many times do I have to tell you...', 'When will you ever learn!?'

Deciding what interventions are appropriate in advance can assist us in being brief, addressing the behaviour calmly, with appropriate assertion. If we need to speak at any length with a student, it is better to do so when he has 'cooled down', quietly aside from the group. Even then keep it brief; a classroom is not the best or most appropriate counselling venue; you may have to refer it to an after-class session.

Loudness and pitch

The time to use a sharp pitch is when one is significantly annoyed or when immediate arousal and *attention* is required (safety, fighting, running on to a road).

Loudness is also to be avoided unless necessary for effect. 'Oi' is entirely appropriate to halt a dangerous cycle of behaviour. I use it when I see a serious fight on playground duty. 'Oi!', then drop the voice to firm and assertive after eye contact and attention is established. There are rare occasions, of course, when teachers will have to use physical restraint until the child regains some self control – see special note below.

Teachers who are regularly loud, on low-level disruptions, tend to have loud classes. They also tend to create a negative 'tone' making it difficult for students to know where the 'weighting' of the teacher's anger lies. (What is worth getting angry over?) Healthy appropriate working noise needs to be discussed at the beginning of the year under 'communication in our classroom'. (See also p. 114.)

Special note on 'physical touching'

In the current social climate teachers have been advised to consider carefully *any* form of 'physical touching' of students in their care, because of concern about both potential litigation (this is rare) and connotations of abuse (also rare).

In social terms it is perceived as more 'ambiguous' when a male teacher touches a student than when a female teacher does so. When female teachers use 'touch' to affirm, praise or reassure, it is normally viewed in the context of nurture and care.

We should distinguish between the use of directional touch to praise or affirm — not inappropriate at lower primary level (see Wheldall 1992) — and touching a child in a situation of actual or potential conflict.

It is also advisable for male teachers to enlist the supportive presence of a female colleague in any one-to-one counselling settings as a basic ethical probity when working with female students.

Physical restraint
The whole issue of the appropriateness of physical touch on the one hand and possible restraint in a crisis should be discussed within the context of a whole-school policy. It should not be left *merely* to professional discretion. Restraining students when they are a danger to themselves or others is not inappropriate and can be covered under the maxim 'appropriate and dutiful care'. In a crisis, though, it is advisable to have a colleague sent for ASAP — where possible.

In a fight, if students refuse to stop after an unambiguous command and if you have managed to direct the audience away and the behaviour of the 'contenders' is still physically dangerous, physical restraint may be necessary, not merely advisable. Of course, this situation is rare, and even rarer is the possibility of litigation. The paramount right is that of safety.

The primary need is to create a playground environment where the fundamental rights of safety and fair treatment are protected by a school-wide policy involving all members of the school community.

Balancing short-term and long-term issues
In class Melissa is seat-wandering and chatting away at another group's table.

T   [Walks over] Melissa what are you doing? [Said pleasantly but expectantly]
S   I'm *only* [only is said sarcastically] getting a pencil from Lisa. [This is probably untrue and said with hand on hip, 'tsk tsks' and sighs]

In the short term the teacher does not address the postural cues and tone; he redirects. (This skill is discussed in detail later in the text.)

T   Maybe you were [still pleasant] and I want you to go back and work at your table, thank you.

The teacher walks off communicating the expectation of compliance allowing 'take-up time' and face-saving. All this is communicated by how the *teacher* is behaving; decisively. Melissa waits several seconds and walks back (exaggeratedly) and mutters en route. She flops into her seat and slowly (oh so slowly) begins work. Just before the bell, the teacher (in drawing the lesson to a close) says to Melissa. 'Melissa, I'd like to see you after class for a moment!' 'Oh! What for?!' (she knows). Here the teacher just directs the class to pack up, 'Chairs under the tables everyone, please, and any bits of litter by your feet in the bin thanks.' The teacher waits by the door for Melissa. Melissa stands sulkily against the wall, arms folded, a scowl on her face.

T   Melissa, in class when I asked you to go back to your table you said [and here the teacher briefly mirrors the student's tone and gesture, 'tongue in cheek'] 'I'm only getting a pencil from Lisa!' Now I don't speak like that to you and I don't like it when you speak like that to me. [This is said quietly, firm eye contact, seriously.]
S   I didn't mean it! [Melissa frowns, looks a little 'guilty'.]
T   Maybe you didn't, but we've got a class agreement about respect and I expect you to use it.
S   All right — but I told you I didn't mean it.
T   OK. You and I have to live in that room. Let's use respect. See you later [smile].

The teacher has been pleasant, but made his point using 'I' messages. It will also minimise secondary behaviour next time in class.

This brief word (after class) re-establishes student and teacher relationships. It also reminds Melissa that the teacher in class let her 'save face' by redirecting rather than 'attacking' her there and then. It doesn't take long, and it can be carried out at any age level.

What to do when...?
In Chapter 4 a suggested range of least to most intrusive repertoire is set out. Special emphasis is given to the 'language of discipline' that can act as an *aide-mémoire*: what to do when?

- What will I do when faced with, say, calling out, butting in, arguing? What approaches will I use? Which is appropriate? What can I say, ought I to say, faced with...?
- When will I intervene? (Timing is important.) Some behaviours need to be nipped in the bud with a decisive direction, others require a more casual approach, and even tactical ignoring is appropriate at times. Some teachers intervene too quickly, too intrusively, while others wait too long and a domino effect occurs. How will I intervene? What level of assertion (voice tone, proximity, postural cues), is appropriate?

In answering these questions we are forming a discipline plan as acute as any lesson plan. It is the balancing of preventative, corrective, consequential and supportive discipline.

BUILDING RELATIONSHIPS

At the heart of effective teaching and discipline is the working relationship between teacher and students. We work from, to and through relationships every time we address a student's behaviour. I've asked countless students, 'What makes a good teacher — a teacher who you'll work well for and who doesn't give you a hard time?' Their answers can be summed up as follows:

- Someone with a sense of humour, who doesn't take everything desperately seriously, who isn't petty;
- Who is fair, doesn't have favourites, gives you a chance;
- Who doesn't make you look stupid in front of your friends (minimises embarrassment, sarcasm, ridicule and the 'cheap shot');
- Who protects your rights and helps you to 'belong' to the group;
- Who will help you with the work (beyond class time if necessary);
- Who makes the work interesting;
- And *most of all* who treats you like a 'person' — an individual and not just a student.

Teaching has never just been about the transmission of knowledge, or the 'controlling' of students. We are in a profession that depends for the quality of teaching and learning as much on the kind of working relationships we can develop as on anything else. This has always been so for effective teachers.

We *have* to discipline students and where the relationship is generally positive it will be easier for the student both to take the correction (and the consequences where appropriate) and to re-establish the working relationship once any bad feelings have subsided. Make it difficult for the student to hate you. We can't make children (or anyone) like us but we can, by our daily treatment, make it difficult for them to dislike us. Simple things like the following:

- Respect a student even when you 'dislike' him or her.
- Model normal courtesies like 'Good-morning', 'Hi, how's it going?' (I've had students grunt to such a greeting on several occasions before finally getting a full-blown 'Hi' and smile back.) Greet them outside the class too.
- *Always* use their first name; make the effort to learn it and use it. When teaching in secondary schools I ask a student to do a seat plan of the class for that day, with first names, so that when I move around I can address students on a more personal level. Most students will give you their first name when asked if we ask pleasantly.
- Ask to see their work when entering their personal space. Rarely will a student refuse. Some students will play the 'over-service me' game by covering their work and saying, 'No! my work's no good' (*et al.*) Redirect this, 'I still want to see it, thanks.' Avoid over-pitying, 'Oh don't say that Rachel, I'm sure it's not. Come on, let me see please.' If they refuse a redirection, leave them with a 'when/ then' direction: 'OK Rachel, when you're ready to show me the work let me know.' Then walk away letting the student own it. After all, you can't *make* them show you the work; forcing them only over-services their attention-seeking. If a pattern of such behaviour occurs we can work with them on a long-term strategy.
- Speak to a student quietly, *aside from the group*, wherever you suspect significant resistance (this approach is only appropriate during 'on-task' time, of course).
- Defer consequences where appropriate rather than force a no-win situation.
- If you say you'll follow up, do it.
- Apologise where you know you're in the wrong.
- Let the whole class know if you're really having a bad day. It avoids giving a mixed message about where your 'bad mood' might be coming from.
- If feasible (certainly at primary levels), remember birthdays and special events.

- Find ways to encourage your students, and make an effort in (and out of) class to say a special word each week to every student. It's worth it.

DEVELOPING A POSITIVE CLASSROOM CLIMATE

There are many preventative aspects to positive management of a class that affect the classroom climate. The teacher is a key player in what emerges as the *characteristic* 'tone'.

- How would you describe your characteristic verbal/non-verbal behaviour when managing and disciplining students? Do you speak calmly, hastily, naggingly, sharply, most of the time? How do you think your students would describe your management style? Ever asked them?
- How clear, fair, enforceable are your rules and consequences. (See pp. 119-125.)
- How do you use encouragement? Do you listen to your students? Do you notice their on-task behaviours as well as their off-task behaviours?
- What is the physical environment like in your room? Although there are often constraints at the secondary level, in what ways could you work with your peers and students to make the working environment more attractive and comfortable to work in? (In many schools we've scrounged carpet, fixed desks, put shelves up, curtains, pot plants, etc. It *does* have an effect.) Is work regularly displayed? (Even if you're in the room for only a few periods in the week — monitors can put it up/take it down.) Are seating arrangements changed or modified for interactive work from time to time?
- How is learning organised? In what way do you cater for mixed abilities? How competitive are your assessment procedures? How descriptive is your assessment? In what way do you give students the opportunity to learn from mistakes or 'poor' work output?
- Do you use humour (not sarcasm) now and then?
- In what way do you plan ahead for likely, or possible, disruptions (especially for the common ones such as talking out of turn, social chit-chat, procrastination, seat-wandering)?
- In what way are you coping for the learning disadvantaged in your groups?
- Are you aware of the preferred learning styles of your students?

Do you vary your teaching and learning approaches? For example, do you utilise small-group work to develop and encourage co-operative learning and social skills? Do you balance group and individual learning approaches?

- What kind of role model are you in class time?
- Are you well prepared, especially with a range of 'work' for early finishers?
- Do you use sarcasm or put downs to 'put students in their place?'
- When you're angry with a student, how do you communicate your anger? Do you separate your anger at his behaviour from him as a person?
- How quickly do you return marked and assessed work (the bane of our lives)?
- What sort of conflict-resolution skills do you (as a teacher) model?

A DISCIPLINE PLAN

- **Gives confidence**. Especially when the pressure is on. We know beforehand how we can proceed in a least to most intrusive way.

- **Gives stability**. We are all subject to vagaries of mood, chance, circumstance. When Michelle is calling out... When Daniel and Paul are having a loud, distracting conversation... When Nick is into task avoidance... It's not easy to be 'creative' when under emotional arousal. Planning ahead for 'inevitable' classroom disruptions will give stability and some consistency to our practice.

- **Helps avoid over-reacting**. Students want their teachers to 'control' them, provided that control is delivered fairly, with dignity and not in a way that *causes* the student to lose face. Students are more likely to co-operate with their teachers when the teacher remains 'calm' and avoids unnecessary (and in some teachers intentional) embarrassment, sarcasm, ridicule, confronting tactics.

You can recall, even as an adult (maybe a rude, intimidating 'boss', or section leader, or principal), how it feels when you are shamed in front of your peers.

'You idiot!!'

'Shut up!!'

'If you sat up straight and paid attention you might learn something...!'

'Wake up! Is there anything in there?' (Here the teacher taps at the student's head.)

'Are you thick or what?!! What did I just say — are you deaf?!'

'What kind of mess do you call this, eh...?! (Teacher pokes at the messy, unmargined work.)

Of course we get frustrated but we don't need to resort to this kind of rubbish to get the message across. It breeds unnecessary resentment, causes the student to feel he has 'lost face' (in front of his peers) and makes long-term workable relationships difficult if not impossible.

Worse: there are teachers for whom, this approach 'works', in that they get 'compliance', but at what cost to self-esteem? Utility is no proof of 'good' management; 'good' requires us to ask a value question about the 'how' as well as the 'what'.

We can be firm and assertive without roughness or sarcasm.

THE RIPPLE EFFECT

(Kounin, 1971) When we discipline a student in a 'public' forum like a classroom we discipline more than the individual (or several), we address the whole class.

If I walk over and intimidate a student chewing gum by making references to 'stupid cow-like actions!'; if I gesticulate with the finger; have a raised or sharp voice... My behaviour will affect the other students nearby. Some will be worried (especially if they're chewing gum); some will laugh out of nervousness ('What are you laughing at?!'); some will, out of a sense of social justice, act as a Greek chorus, 'What are you picking on her for? It's only chewing gum!', 'You keep out of this, it's got nothing to do with you!'

This teacher–student transaction 'ripples' out and is felt, perceived, differentially by the class. These kind of scenarios happen, unfortunately, and 'bad day' notwithstanding, some teachers alienate even the co-operative members of the class by the way they characteristically discipline. As the Elton Report (1989, p. 69) notes:

A discipline plan sets pupil relationships (teacher–student, teacher-class, pupil-pupil) as a goal just as important as teaching and learning goals.

A CLASSROOM DISCIPLINE PLAN

It is important at the establishment phase of the year to have in place a 'plan' for classroom discipline. A plan is a consistent approach through prevention, strategy and support to minimise unnecessary disruption and take appropriate 'short' and 'longer-term' measures to correct disruptive behaviour patterns.

Preventative action (to prevent or minimise unnecessary disruption)

- Have an aesthetically pleasing and functional room
- Prepare and utilise appropriate materials
- Arrive at class on time
- Plan interesting lessons (as much as possible)
- Cater (and plan) for mixed abilities
- Plan appropriate seating arrangements
- Plan for the language of discipline (what you say and when)
- Make clear the routines
- Have clear, fair, positive rules and known consequences for significant rule-breaking

In developing a classroom discipline plan

- State rules positively where possible
- Explain/discuss reasons for the rule
- Discuss related consequences for breaking rules
- Acknowledge, affirm, positive behaviour

Corrective action (the actions you take when disruptive behaviour occurs; least to most intrusive)

- *Tactical ignoring* (where appropriate)
- *Simple, brief directions* (finish with thank you, or please)
- *Rule reminders* (simple reminder or restatement about the class rules)
- *Simple choice* ('in bag or on my desk, thank you')
- *Casual or direct question* (avoid 'why?', what are you doing/what should you be doing?)
- *Redirect* (instead of arguing)
- *Make consequences clear* (via 'choice')
- *Direct student to work aside* (from peers in room)
- *Cool-off time*
- *Exit/time out* (for dangerous behaviour, or continual disruption, or safety issue)

Protocols of discipline

When carrying out corrective action teacher should:

- Maintain eye contact
- Minimise embarrassment and hostility
- Use respectful but assertive tone of voice
- Pick up on-task behaviour, acknowledge
- Privately encourage positive behaviours
- Watch spatial proximity
- Avoid unnecessary argument
- Give clear 'choices' to maximise students' responsibility
- Be consistent in follow through
- Utilise wide support

Supportive action (action to employ support for teacher and student)

Time-out: A cooling-off period, or withdrawal under supervision.

Contracting/counselling: Any process to lead to behaviour agreement and behaviour recovery.

Formal support processes: Parent conference, welfare and psychological services.

SUMMARY

In developing a discipline plan, then, you will need to have:

- Established your fair, clear, **rules** and exactions.
- Thought through the obvious **routines** that make a class run well (from entering and leaving and pack-up routines through to use of monitors). Ask the basic questions such as: How can I have a smooth entry and exit? How can I gain their attention without shouting or nagging? How can I hold their attention during instructional or administration time? How can I distribute tasks, materials, smoothly? How can I *retrieve* attention when I need it? Effective management is not accidental it has to be planned.
- Discussed central **consequences** for significant rule infringement. With older students (middle and upper) the emphasis is on *rights* infringement (see p. 108).
- Developed a 'least to most' **aide mémoire** for corrective discipline. Be aware of what you'll say when faced with common disruptive behaviours. Write it down, practise it, make it yours.
- Thought carefully about being aware of **matching** your corrective intervention with the degree of disruption displayed by the student.

In any one lesson we will be tactically ignoring one or more students and directing or reminding another, and for those students tactical ignoring and a brief reminder/direction will be enough. Yet others will need redirecting or even a consequence to call them to 'own' their own behaviour. An *aide mémoire* will enable us to move up and down our conscious repertoire of teacher skills according to the degree of disruption. That is the value of a *plan*.

4

The Language of Discipline

You'll read a number of 'scripts' outlining common discipline scenarios between teachers and students. Imagine yourself in these situations and try saying the 'teacher parts': the language of discipline.

Try modifying your tone of voice. Congruence between tone and content is important. Does your tone express hostility, aggression, sarcasm, pleading or assertion (decisiveness)? Try adding a relaxed, decisive, assertive posture and you'll see how tone and gesture dramatically 'weight' our language.

The 'language of discipline' is best set in the context of least to most intrusive depending on the situation and degree of intrusion by the student's behaviour. (see Fig. 2).

TACTICAL IGNORING OF BEHAVIOUR

Blind ignorance is never useful, it can even be dangerous, but *tactical* ignoring can be an appropriate teacher response to some misbehaviour, for example:

- sulking
- a student's whiney, sulky, tone of voice
- a student's 'non-compliant' body language (the pout, the eyes to ceiling, the dumb insolent head down, the sibilant sigh)
- some calling out (if just one or two)
- some tantrum behaviours
- butting in, silly comments, or clowning

We ought not to ignore any safety issues, potential physical danger, *any* sort of abuse (racial, 'put downs', sexual harassment), blatant intimidation.

Tactical ignoring is a difficult skill but can be very effective. Students are not silly, they can even pick up what we're doing. However, they may get worse before they slow down their behaviour. One of my colleagues was tactically ignoring a difficult student, who then came up and whispered in her ear, 'If you ignore me, I'll get worse.' The

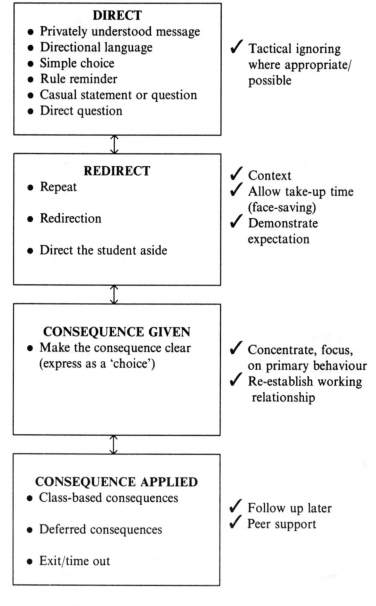

DIRECT
- Privately understood message
- Directional language
- Simple choice
- Rule reminder
- Casual statement or question
- Direct question

✓ Tactical ignoring where appropriate/ possible

REDIRECT
- Repeat

- Redirection

- Direct the student aside

✓ Context
✓ Allow take-up time (face-saving)
✓ Demonstrate expectation

CONSEQUENCE GIVEN
- Make the consequence clear (express as a 'choice')

✓ Concentrate, focus, on primary behaviour
✓ Re-establish working relationship

CONSEQUENCE APPLIED
- Class-based consequences

- Deferred consequences

- Exit/time out

✓ Follow up later
✓ Peer support

Fig. 2. Language of discipline: least to most intrusive

difficulty in its use lies in the frustration we experience as a result of attention-seeking behaviour. We feel we *have* to respond, but sometimes *not* responding may be more appropriate. Jason is clicking his fingers, 'Eh, Miss, Miss!' He knows the rule. If we regularly say 'Don't call out!', 'Shh' or, as bad, *just answer* on application of his attention-seeking we may overly reinforce it.

Tactical ignoring can carry the message that *that* kind of behaviour is unacceptable. It gives the student a private cue. It says, in effect, 'I will answer you *when* you put your hand up!' If several students are calling out then a general direction or *general* rule reminder is appropriate. Tactical ignoring works best on the individual student.

It needs to be actively balanced with encouragement. When the student puts a hand up (on task) without noise, 'Yes Paul, see your hand up. Thanks. Be with you in a sec.' Effective directional eye-scanning is part of tactical ignoring — the ability to see several behaviours at any one time. It is a skill that needs to be developed, especially in picking up the on-task behaviours to reinforce and encourage.

We can often combine tactical ignoring with directional language or rule reminders. 'Sam, we've got a rule for asking questions, use it, thank you'. Here the teacher looks away (take-up time) and reinforces students with their hands up. She then tactfully ignores Sam's further calling out. Melissa whines to the teacher, pulling her skirt 'Mees!! Meeeees!' The teacher uses a when/then statement. 'When you ask properly (remember?), then I'll answer you.' The teacher then turns away and tactically ignores until the student makes an effort at non-whining.

Give a reminder, 'Sam, I want you to go back to your seat and work there, thanks.' Sam goes but has to make a silly noise on the way, walk in an exaggerated fashion, then flop down and sigh. He pouts for a few minutes then slowly (oh so slowly) gets back to work. The teacher tactically ignores the 'route march' (*et al.*) and reinforces the on-task work at the desk. Later (longer term) she can work on the attitude behind the 'secondary behaviours'; when the audience isn't around. You don't change attitudes by public lectures in front of a child's peers.

The key to tactical ignoring is our attitude and our goal. The attitude is not to be smart and tactically clever but to convey a 'when/then' aspect to the ignoring. Decide for yourself (and by discussion with colleagues):

- what behaviours you can appropriately ignore;

- whether you can tolerate low-level attention-seeking;
- how long (with any behaviour) you're prepared to tactically ignore;
- what steps will follow your tactical ignoring.

PRIVATELY UNDERSTOOD MESSAGES

These are well-understood cues that convey expectation, a simple message, annoyance, an intent, approval. Facial messages: the wink, frown, nod, raised eyes, even the smile. The 'blocking' hand when a student butts in. Putting a hand up (lower primary age) as a signal to remind for hands up (rather than calling out). The 'OK' sign with index finger and thumb signals 'well done' or 'on target'. The beckoning hand to call the student across the room. The peace sign, the mock salute, even a hand shake. The 'time-out' sign (a 'T' made with two hands).

In a recent English lesson (with Year 9s) I was discussing non-verbal communication. Using the come-over-here beckoning signal, I said to Kelvin 'What does that signal communicate?' 'Up you,' he said with a sly grin. I then did it with the curled index finger (rather than the second finger). 'Oh, *that* means come here — got ya now!' We need to use the right cue!

Body language generally is a powerful communicator. If we *characteristically* slouch, glare, point, sigh and raise our eyes to the ceiling, march around, crowd a student's personal space, look vacant or bored or indifferent, we send a message. It's worth *consciously* aiming for some congruence between *what* we say, *how* we say it, and the package — our postural cues and gestures:

- non-intimidating, non-threatening (save intimidation for the extremely rare times when physical intervention is necessary);
- confidence in tone;
- directional eye contact (not wavering and unstable);
- proximity — watch 'personal space' (we know how it feels when somebody encroaches on our 'personal space');
- upright but relaxed posture;
- open hand when gesturing; avoid pointing at a student in a gesticulating way — imagine a finger in your facial proximity! Open hand is less threatening.

These are the elements of an assertive stance.

DIRECTIONS TO INDIVIDUALS OR SMALL GROUPS

Be brief, avoid over-correcting. When students are being disruptive it's a plain fact of life that they won't listen to long-winded tirades or speeches.

Direct to the behaviour you want to see (the appropriate behaviour). Keep the direction short and to the point. It can be helpful to write out the sorts of directions you want to use so that the language comes out as positive as possible. Use 'do' messages, instead of 'don't' messages; save 'don't' for when you really need it.

Rephrase negatives
The correctional can still *sound* positive:

- 'Don't forget to pack up the blocks,' 'Don't forget to put the toys away' can become 'Remember to put the blocks away' (beckon).
- 'Remember to put the chairs under the table. Thanks.'
- 'Don't walk away from the mess!' can become 'OK everyone — look this way (eye contact) let's beat the clock to pack up time. 1, 2...'
- 'No you can't' becomes 'When...then'.
- 'Don't run' becomes 'Walk quietly'.
- When children (in primary) want to go to another activity without cleaning up first, use 'Yes, when you've cleaned up the maths blocks' (or, 'after... then...').
- 'Don't butt in!' becomes 'One at a time, thanks' or 'Waiting, thank you' (use a privately understood signal, a 'block' hand).
- 'Ben, hands up (positive) without calling out, please' the negative follows the more important positive. Allow 'take-up time' by refocussing on someone else with a hand up. This removes the over-servicing of possible attention-seeking.

Craig had his foot up and was leaning back on his chair, bit of a sly grin. I established brief eye contact with the use of his name. Briefly (from 'up front') 'Craig, feet down, thanks.' The 'thanks' is added both to soften the direction, so it doesn't sound like too much of a 'big deal', and to add *expectation*. All the points noted earlier about 'tone' are also relevant; positive, firm, even a fun tone, a wink, can be appropriate. Use the hand (open) to beckon 'foot down'. If this had happened during on-task time I would have simply walked close beside and said, 'Craig, feet down thanks, let's have a look at your work' (distract and divert).

If students are leaning back on their chairs:

'Mike, four on the floor, thanks.'
'Ben, sitting up thank you', or even a casual question used as a distraction.
'Ben, how's your work going?' (He sits up as you come over.)

These simple questions (where positive) are more appropriate than:

'Don't lean back on your chair like that! They cost money!' (What furniture that we use in classrooms ever costs a lot of money?!)
'Is that what you do at home! Eh?!' 'Yeah!', says Ben.

'I' statements
Used as directions, these personalise the transaction

'Carl, I want you to keep the noise down, thanks, we're trying to work over here.'
'I want you to put the scissors away now, please.'
'I want you to use the equipment properly, thanks.'
'I want you to work back at your table now, thank you.'

We can often combine rule reminders with directions. Many of our directions act as reminders anyway.

'Paul and Wayne, you know the safety rule. Use the ... properly, please.'
'Lisa and Michelle, I want you to face this way and listen, thank you'.

As a synonym for 'I' statements with upper secondary:

'Do me the courtesy of facing this way and listening, thanks.'
'When you're talking I can't make my point, I'd like you to (or I need you to) face this way and listen. Thank you.'

Like most directional language, the *way* it's said will be important.

Directional language and small children
Brevity, simplicity and clarity are essential ingredients when directing small children. Michael, a five-year-old, is the slowest packer-upper.
    'Michael, I want you to pack up the blocks in the tray now.' Teacher

points and adds 'Thanks'. 'But, but...Lisa didn't do her blocks!' he whines. Teacher doesn't buy into this, she redirects. Motioning to the box she repeats instead of arguing.

One of the key aspects of discipline for small children is the training element. Our job is to lead, guide and positively remind regularly. One day they'll do the responsible behaviour without being reminded — then you faint!

- Keep directions focused and simple. Balance the positive/negative aspects of the direction.
  'Walk quietly (no running).'
  'Hands up (without calling out).'
  'Face the front (wink), no talking, thank you.'
- Stay calm and keep a firm expectant tone.
- Not too close (overbearing) but a touch on the arm can help.
- Repeat if necessary and encourage when they comply.
  'Eyes this way' (to several).
  'David, hands up' (teacher puts hand over mouth) 'and quiet mouth' (here she smiles, saying the last bit more quietly).

If students argue, answer back, want the last word or refuse, we need to redirect. This is covered in some detail later.

Normally, discipline transactions are best dealt with by least (and positive) intrusive measures first *before* moving to more intrusive.

In the music class, Year 7s, the teacher is 'orchestrating' several groups working with basic percussion instruments. Nigel is tapping his claves instead of waiting.

T   Wait thanks, Nigel. [Brief eye contact and the teacher resumes the lesson flow. Keeping the 'flow' is important in whole-group teaching.]

T   [To Ben who shakes his tambourine] Ben, rest, thanks. [She beckons a downward motion with her hand — that's all. No big speech. Then 'take-up' time.]

T   [To the whole class] Everyone [a little louder], instruments down, Nigel and team, your go.

This 'orchestrational' directive language is focused, direct, positive. The teacher also encourages positive behaviour. 'That's better Paul, good timing.' 'Nice beat, well done Nick.' 'Thanks for waiting Tom — it helps.'

T   One at a time, Paul. [This to Paul who is butting in over another student]
T   Richard, four on the floor, thank you. [This to a student heavily leaning back and turning around. The teacher speaks briefly, beckons him to sit forward with her hand, and again resumes the 'flow' of the lesson.]

Anyone watching 'merely' sees a good lesson. However, the discipline language, and how it is used is part of this teacher's plan.

DIRECTIONAL 'CHOICES'

Adam has food on his desk. He's secreting crisps into class. Rather than use most intrusive measures, 'Right! Give them to me! C'mon!' or just straight snatching, we can put the onus back to the student.

'Adam, nice crisps but (I want you to put them) in your bag or on my desk' (the 'I statement' can be added or left out). Sometimes we can preface the choice ('in/on') by a casual disclaimer, 'Nice Walkman Pete; you know the rule, in your bag or on my desk — ta'. Walk away *as if* to communicate that their compliance is naturally forthcoming.

Nick is six, he's got a little car on his table, he's 'brmm, brmming'. 'Nice car, Nick, racing car... where do you want to put it, in your tray or on my desk?' Ninety per cent put it in their bag or tray. If they argue we redirect rather than make it a fight.

T   Jeremy, I want you to put the Walkman in your bag or on my desk.
S   Oh, I wasn't listening to it! [Sulky look, marginal eye contact, imputation of unfairness — Oh cruel world!]
T   Maybe you weren't, but I want you to put it in your bag or on my desk. [Redirection, nor argument.]
S   But other teachers let us have 'em! Don't they Mike? [To another student who says 'Yeah!']
T   [The teacher doesn't argue.] Maybe they do, but here the rule is clear, in your bag or on my desk.

The teacher's eye contact is direct, the tone positive but assertive. She walks away leaving the impression that the student is clearly *expected* to do it. She hasn't argued, she has redirected, keeping the focus on the primary issue.

As she walks away allowing a 'take-up time' (she still has oblique eye contact), Jeremy huffily walks over to his bag and puts it away, still exuding residual pouting. As he goes back to work the teacher walks over and says, 'Thanks for putting it away, how's your work going?' This re-establishes the *working* relationship.

It could have been different:

T	Get that Walkman off your desk now.
S	C'mon, I wasn't listening to it!
T	I don't care! Do as I say!
S	But other teachers...
T	I don't care if every teacher in this school lets you have a Walkman, I just said get it away — are you deaf?! Get it off your desk.
S	But...! [Teacher snatches it up and refuses to give it back at the end of the lesson, increasing the conflict.]

When/then

Another form of direction is the use of the 'conditional choice'.

Melissa (bit of a wag) calls out at the beginning of the lesson, 'Can I go to the toilet?' The teacher suspects it's a ploy. Of course, the 'audience' is watching.

T	*When* I've finished this part of the lesson *then* you can go. Sure. [The teacher then resumes the lesson.]

This conditional direction is another way of giving a 'delayed yes'. It avoids unnecessary confrontation.

T	No you can't go to the toilet, I'm teaching!
T	Why do you want to go now? Why didn't you go before, we've only just started the lesson?

When students thrust their work in your personal space, while you're helping others: 'Can you check this?!' says Rod. 'Sure, when you're back in your seat Rod.'

Steve calls out across the room during on-task time, while I'm working with a group of students. Although I could *tactically* ignore, I choose to use a conditional direction. 'Steve, when you've got your hand up without calling out, I'll come over.' When he has his hand up appropriately, wait a moment and reinforce: 'See your hand up Steve, ta. Be there in a moment.'

When *establishing* learning procedures it is important to explain and discuss how you want students to seek your assistance. This will vary according to subject.

RULE REMINDERS

This is simply reminding about or restating the known and established rule/s. One can't use this approach (of course) if there are no established class rules, conventions or agreements.

T   Paul, we've got a rule for class discussion, use it thanks.

T   You know *our* rule for safety, use it please.

If the student argues, redirect (see pp. 87-9).

Some class rules are bound by school-wide rules, some are specific to that subject area. If there is a school-wide rule for eating in class, walking in corridors, reasonable uniform codes, reasonable language codes, we can *simply* remind. There can be caveats to rules of course: we do eat in class on *special* occasions, have cassette recorders on *special* occasions, have non-uniform days.

It is important, though, for all staff to support the fair rules by positive reminders and encouragement where they are kept.

If a student argues the toss:

T   Dave, we've got a rule about gum, in the bin thank you.

S   Oh, c'mon. It's a bit of a dumb rule innit?! [Here he leans back in mock provocation and sighs.]

T   Maybe you think it is [tune in] but it's the school rule, in the bin please.

S   Not doing anything wrong. S'not a major crime is it?!

T   No [tune in] it's a school rule [wink] in the bin thanks. [There the teacher walks away giving 'take-up' time. Most will sigh and drop it in the bin.]

If the student is still chewing five minutes later give a choice/ consequence (see p. 90).

Rule reminders can also be expressed as questions. 'What's *our* rule for...?' 'Can you remember *our* rule for...?'

DISTRACTIONS AND DIVERSIONS

The teacher begins a new unit on copper sulphate crystals. 'OK everyone, today we'll be looking at how we can grow crystals...' Before he can finish the class wag calls out, 'Ohhh! we done that in Year 6!' The teacher doesn't even look at the student who has butted in (he tactically ignores that), he diverts by asking a general question. 'OK, who has done this experiment before?' Two or three call out with their hands up, the teacher gives a brief, general rule reminder: 'OK folks, remember our rule for asking questions. Yes Paul?' Here he turns to a boy with his hand up... The teacher has kept a positive lesson flow by diverting the butting-in comment.

- We can ask a question as a form of diversion, when a few students are talking while you are giving up-front instruction.
- We can ask for assistance from potential disruptors. I'll often ask a student to hold a chart, or help me with a display or activity.
- Invite another student to work with a troublesome student.
- We can divert by moving close to a child during 'on-task' time.
- Asking questions about the work is itself a form of distraction. If a student has a picture of a pop star on their diary or exercise book I often have a brief chat about so and so (this is 'low-budget' relationship building). This brief distraction acts as a preface to a general redirection.
- If you suspect an escalating pattern of disruption you can divert by directing the student to work away from the other students.
- One of my colleagues uses a 'sanity' diversion to direct the annoying disruptive student out of the room for ten minutes or so. She directs the student to take the 'library tag' (a postcard-sized plywood tag with the classroom number on) to the library. This is a form of time out, more so for the teacher! The student thinks he is being sent for a job. This approach is best used earlier in the disruptive cycle, rather than later. It also relies on the peer-support of the librarian!
- Working in a science classroom with a very disturbed Year 7 student (who was kicking furniture, and being very silly with science equipment as well as hassling other students), I decided to direct him from the room. Realising that he probably wouldn't come I chose to distract and divert. Leaving the classroom door open, I walked out and in a loud voice said, 'I wonder if Michael has any A4 or writing paper in his bag?' I said this because he'd told me earlier he couldn't do the work because he had no paper. He was out of the classroom in a shot! Once out, I closed the door and said 'OK Mike, before we go back in I need to have a quick chat...'

Directing the student aside in class

If a student comes into class late, rather than start a big 'third degree' about late passes, have a brief word such as 'OK David, take a seat, I'll check it out with you later.' When the instructional phase of the lesson is finished, then you can direct the student aside from the group and have a brief chat about his lateness. Of course, if there is a pattern of lateness we'll follow that up, outside class time, rather than 'publicly' question (and unnecessarily embarrass) the student.

If a student tends to 'tap dance' within his little coterie it can be helpful to discipline him away from the group. Direct him aside by casually calling him over.

T   Ian, see you for a moment over here, thanks.
S   [Ian swaggers over.] Yeah [sigh] what do you want? [He folds his arms in closed body language.]

In directing the student across the room for a brief chat, the teacher acts *as if* the student will come by firmly (not loudly) directing the student with a beckoning hand; the teacher then resumes whatever activity she was engaged in (sending the signal that she expects him to come over). If he doesn't she'll go through this brief exercise again. 'Ian, see you for a moment, thank you.'

This teacher action is a form of 'split attention'. While working with a group of students at one table I see William being silly at the other table. Rather than walk away from the students I'm currently helping I direct across the tables to William.

I can either give a brief direction from a distance ('William, back to work please, I'll come and check it in a moment') or call him across away from the group and ask him what he's doing (direct question).

Wherever possible we are trying to keep our discipline at the least intrusive level. When Ian comes over the teacher can then direct, remind or question him about his behaviour.

Deflective statements

Where a student comes into class visibly angry or upset, the teacher can usefully acknowledge the student's emotive state and supportively redirect.

Rather than 'Don't come into my class with that look on your face!' the teacher will say something like, 'I can see you're upset, Michelle. Other students are trying to work. If you want to cool off take a seat over there. OK?'

S   Gees Miss! This work is really dumb — it's so gross! [The student looks frustrated. He's probably struggling with the work, or he could be having a bad day.]

T   I can see you're uptight Nick, but that's our set work. How can I help you? [Or] Can I give you a hand?

If the student is particularly upset you can allow him cool-off time in or out of the room as is appropriate.

I sometimes direct the student right outside the room door open — just outside. 'Look Dave, what's up? I can see you're upset. You're not normally like this. I've asked you to settle down, if you're having a bad day, OK, but others are trying to work. OK? Ready to come back in or do you need some cool-off time?

Any directing aside essentially 'privatises' as much of the discipline as possible.

USING QUESTIONS

If a couple of students are talking animatedly a teacher could easily over-react by coming in at the most intrusive level: 'OK you two, you know you're not supposed to be talking — how many times have I told you, eh?!' Any approach like this is bound to get their 'backs up'. With 'low-level' disruption (vacant time-wasting; 'fiddlers'; those who appear not to know what to do; off-task 'gas-bagging', a teacher can minimise escalating the behavioural outcome by a casual question. Move alongside the students and ask the question in a casual, even disinterested way (not uninterested):

T   How's it going Paul?

T   Well Mike, how's the work going?

T   Lisa and Michelle, having problems?

T   [To two students discussing a TV show] Lisa and Michelle [wink] I'm sure it's a nice programme but how's your maths going?

T   Adrian, can I see your work, please?

This gives a non-intrusive cue. Many students will recognise this gambit and say 'Oh, I'm just gunna start, OK?' 'Yes, I know, I'm just reminding you. I'll come back [wink] and see how you're getting on later.'

Where several students are in low-level off-task behaviour, eye-sweep the group, direct eye contact to the main 'contender' and casually ask, 'OK how's it going everyone?'

Of course, if students procrastinate we can use redirection as a way of keeping the focus on the task, the fair rule, the fair right...

In the playground I walked up to students surrounded by litter. Three had their feet up on the round 'café' tables. As I came close one put his feet down. 'Hi fellas, how's it going?' 'S'alright' 'Fair bit of litter here.' 'S'not ours.' 'I'm sure it's not... c',mon, give us a hand to clean it up.' I beckoned him up. Slug-like and with sibilant sigh, we cleaned it all up. 'Ta.' The casual question can often act as a preface to further directions, or questions. Casual questions work best when we have a positive, workable relationship with the students.

DIRECT QUESTIONS

T　　Melissa, you're out of your seat. What are you doing? [This is said casually, non-threateningly (even pleasantly).]

S　　Nothing. [Most students reply with 'nothing', some will go on the defensive.]

T　　[The teacher gives some direct, brief feedback and then follows with a secondary question.] What are you supposed to be doing? [Or 'What should you be doing?' This challenges the student to focus on — and own — the appropriate behaviour.]

The student may well argue when questioned: Sean and Paul are talking loudly, and are into task avoidance (during on-task time). The teacher casually walks over and says:

T　　Sean, Paul [direct eye-contact] what are you two doing?

S　　Nothing. [Here they add postural cues such as sighing and eyes to the ceiling.]

T　　[The teacher concentrates on the issue at hand.] You're talking loudly and I'm trying to work over there with Lisa and Michelle — *what are you supposed to be doing*? [This question refocuses.]

S　　[The students immediately 'raise the banner'.] We're not the only ones talking. What about them over there?

T　　I'm speaking to you. [The teacher is still calm, but direct.] What are you supposed to be doing?

S   [One of the pair says, with light sarcasm] Our work!

T   OK. I expect you to do your work, if you need my help let me know. I'll come and check later. [The teacher walks away — she may choose to have a word with the pair after class.]

The key to this approach is to keep the focus on the central (rather than the side) issues. For example, the same question (used in a hostile way) with a focus on 'secondary' issues could see an outcome not unlike this:

T   What are you two doing!

S   Nothing!

T   You were talking loudly! Now *what* are you *supposed* to be doing? [The teacher's body language is tense, he's close to the two, his index finger is wagging as he emphasises the interrogative.]

S   Anyway, we're not the only ones talking, geee!!

T   [The teacher waves his arm behind him and says] Come on now, who else is talking loudly, who who — come on?!

S   Yeah, well not now but the other days the girls were — you don't pick on them do you?!

T   Don't tell me who I do and don't pick on!!! [And on it goes.]

The teacher has been drawn by secondary issues, which at *this point* are not relevant.

During a science lesson, recently, I saw (in one of the many eye-scans of the room) Robert being silly with a thin rubber hose. Walking over casually I asked:

T   What are you doing?

S   Nothing [Grinning, he'd put the hose down by now.]

T   [Give brief feedback.] Actually I noticed you flicking it around — what are you supposed to be doing? [The secondary question puts the responsibility on the student to tell you.]

S   The experiment thing here.

T   OK [Friendly tone, eyes on the experimental equipment.] How are you going to set it up?

The 'discipline' moves from the direct (but non-confronting) questions back to the teaching issue quickly, cleanly, even positively. If the situation is in any way significantly infringing safety codes we can use a firm rule reminder.

If the student gives a smart reply to the primary question — 'What are you doing?' — it is better to redirect:

T   What are you doing?
S   What's it look like?
T   It looks like... [Be specific. Avoid a sarcastic *bon mot*.] What are you supposed to be doing?
S   I dunno!
T   [The teacher will merely redirect.] You're supposed to be doing your work. Can I help?
S   Nope!
T   OK, when you need my help let me know. [This leaves the ball back in the student's court where it belongs.]

We can't (in the immediate short term) change their thinly disguised hostility; attitude change is best tackled with such students away from their immediate audience — later. Long term we need to show the student we are not their 'enemy'. In the short term we can assertively, but politely, redirect.

Lisa is out of her seat, time-wasting.

T   Lisa [casual and quiet] what are you doing?
S   I'm *only* getting something from Michelle — is that a crime!
T   No, but what are you supposed to be doing?
S   I told you I was just...
T   I know, but what are you supposed to be doing? [The teacher is firm, decisive but not provocative.]
S   My work. [The student says this in a 'sing-song' voice.]
T   [The teacher tactically ignores the tone and postural cues, and redirects.] OK, Lisa, I expect you to go back [smile]. I'll come over and see how it's going later. Thank you.

If the teacher feels and believes the student's tone is particularly rude it can help to punctuate the redirection with a firm quiet 'I' statement.

T   I don't speak like that to you Lisa, and I don't want (or expect) you to speak like that to me — I want you to go back to your seat now.

When using direct questions we need to remember all the guiding principles noted earlier. There is no special strength in prepared language repertoire alone. Tone, proximity, context, expectation, take-up time and re-establishing with the student when he or she is back on task are all essential features of total discipline.

Avoid 'why' questions (especially the negative 'why'):

'Why are you two being stupid over here?!'
'Why haven't you started work yet?'
'Why are you two talking?'
'Why can't you work together without arguing?'
'I've told you a hundred times to...!'

AN ASSERTIVE STATEMENT OR DIRECTION

We can state our concern, our feelings, about the students' behaviour in a decisive, firm, direct way. Distinguish between the student and his behaviour and make your feelings about the issue clear and then redirect. The degree of assertion (and emotion) will depend on the degree of the rights-affecting behaviour.

T   Paul! I don't speak like that to you. I don't want (or expect) you to speak like that to me.

When directing 'up front':

T   Michelle and Louise, I can't teach when you're talking, I want you to face this way and listen thank you.

The concentration is on the effect of the others' behaviour. 'I' statements or messages are the safest, least intrusive way of doing it. We don't need to use the personal pronoun *per se*, we can imply it:

T   Lisa and Paula do me the courtesy of facing this way and listening thank you.

If this is said politely, with expectation, it is effective — especially with older adolescent students.

REDIRECTION

Redirection has been discussed elsewhere in this text (see pp. 25-9). The emphasis of redirection is to keep the *focus on the 'primary'* rather than the 'secondary' issues. Some students are masters at diverting the issues away from the rules, rights or others or your fair directions. Rick and Michael are clearly time-wasting and into heavy social 'chit-chat'.

T   Michael and Rick, I want you to keep the noise down, thanks, and get back to work. [This is said pleasantly but decisively; on a good day a wink and a smile is added!]
S   We're only talking about the work.
T   Maybe you were [the teacher 'dignifies' the 'side' issue] but I want you to keep the noise down and back to work. Thank you.

If, however, I say, 'I don't care what you were talking about!' this only adds fuel to the escalating conflict. A brief dignifying says 'I hear what you say, but....' It refocuses.

At this point the teacher walks away to allow 'take-up time' and communicate expectation. Rick wants a last word, 'What about Lisa and Michelle, they were talking too?' As a throw-away line the teacher says, 'And I want you to keep the noise down and back to work.' Rick grunts and says 'yeah, yeah' in a little sing-song voice.

Redirection is a difficult skill in that our natural reaction is often to challenge, argue or debate with the student on the secondary issues.

David was trying to 'break' a clave (a small wooden stick) in music class. I had the students working in groups. He couldn't really break it, he was just being silly. I directed him aside.

T   David, what are you doing?
S   Nothing.
T   I saw you trying to break the clave. [Feedback]
S   But I didn't break it, did I? [Years ago if a student had said this I would have said, 'What has that got to do with it?! It is so easy to get caught up into the student's last word.]
T   Maybe you didn't ['dignify', i.e. briefly acknowledge, it] but what are you supposed to be doing with the clave? [This redirects.]

Like any skill, redirection needs practice.

S   Other teachers let us eat in class.
T   Maybe they do. In this class the rule is clear, in your bag or on my desk, thank you Paul.
S   It's a dumb rule! [Says Debbie when directed to put the chewing gum in the bin.]

T   You could be right (the 'dignifying'] but it's the school rule [wink], in the bin thanks. [The redirection.]

With some secondary students who are not afraid of being 'up front'; their challenging replies *seem* like an attack on our status:

T   Denise, nice crisps, but you know the school rule. In your bag or on my desk. Thank you. [Directed simple choice.]
S   Get real, s'only a few crisps. C'mon!
T   You're right [dignify] but it's a school rule — in your bag or on my desk. Ta [as you walk away].
S   I don't like you — you're not as nice as the teacher we had last year! [A sulky, guilt-inducing piece of teacher-baiting.]
T   Yes, I might not be as nice as your teacher last year [smile] but I'm your teacher this year. How can I help you?

This pleasant *short-term* response is enough; the teacher can privately chat with the student about his attitude later if necessary.

With upper primary and secondary students it is appropriate to walk away to allow take-up time and *act* as if:

- it's no big deal,
- and you're not going to get caught up in a big debate on side issues, and
- the discussion is over.

The walking away is a tactical move also; you keep the general eye-scanning as you *tactically* ignore their muttering.

My rule of thumb is to redirect two or three times at the most. (Where possible allow take-up time.) If after a few minutes they haven't:

— put the food away;
— turned down their loud talking;
— gone back to their place;
— put materials away, or aren't using them appropriately...

then give a directed consequence. If appropriate (i.e. during on-task time) direct the student aside to redirect.

DIRECTED CONSEQUENCE

The use of related consequences is discussed in Chapter 6. In a classroom or group setting if a student continues in a pattern of disruptive behaviour we need to make the consequence clear. In the classroom there are limited *consequences* that we can utilise beyond verbal directions, reminders and redirections. We can:

- Direct them to work away from others in the room as a short-term consequence.
- At lower primary level, direct them to cool-off time in the room when they are significantly affecting learning or safety rights.
- Deprive of equipment when it is being used in an unsafe or disruptive way.
- Use deferred consequences — where we follow up at a later stage.
- Impose 'time out' away from the classroom, the most intrusive short-term consequence (see Chapter 5).

Choice
Prior to applying a consequence it is normally appropriate to give a 'choice'. The 'choice' acts as a last warning and may see the student come back on task.

T   Kathy and Lisa, if you continue to work noisily, I'll have to ask one of you to work away from here. [The teacher points away to another table.]
S   [Kathy looks up sulkily. After all, she's been directed once, and possibly redirected and has now 'owned' her behaviour or remembered to respect others' rights.] We're not the only table that's noisy. [She folds her arms and huffs.]
T   [It is important to act as if you are placing ownership back on them in a non-threatening but firm way. No raised voices, we're not there to make them feel small in front of their peers.] I'm speaking to you, here. If you can't work quietly here I'll have to ask you to work separately. [Avoid phrases like 'I'll *make* you move.' We cannot simply *make* a student move or do anything actually.]

Some teachers may feel this is not a 'real' choice; it is a 'choice' *within* the fair classroom rights and rules. The 'choice' acts as a reminder to responsibility — avoid any arguing.

- When using 'choices' we put responsibility back on the student.
- The student is challenged to *think* about his or her behaviour.

- Emphasising 'choice' in effect says to students that they are the active agent, not merely the 'victim'.
- A 'choice' acts as a conditional warning.

Consequence and follow up

If the student 'chooses' not to settle, direct her to the consequence previously stated. 'Kathy, I want you to take your books and work over there.' If the student argues, calmly redirect, and walk towards the 'spare' desk/table as if she will come. This allows a little face-saving. If she chooses not to come, leave the student with a *deferred* consequence, 'If you choose not to work away, you are choosing to see me at recess.'

'Don't care!' Kathy sulkily has a last word. Resist the temptation to attack this last word, 'You will care!!! I'll see you care!!' Tactically ignore it and follow up later. The follow up will do the convincing. Decide beforehand on a reasonable deferred consequence (for example the 4W from p. 92) or you can ask the student what she thinks she can do about her loud talking (or whatever) in class.

'What are you doing (in class) that's against our fair rules (older students — that affects our class rights and agreements)?'
'Is there any problem in working by the fair rules?'
'Can you come up with a plan to work better in class?'
'How can I help?'

At secondary level it's difficult to find time to follow up at this level of questioning. It will be necessary to follow up at a scheduled time, perhaps with year level co-ordinator support. If you use the school's detention system it can be instructive for the student (if she can write), the subject teacher and co-ordinator to have a 4W form filled in. It gives right of reply as well as the opportunity to offer a way of fixing the behaviour.

If we have had to direct a student back more than three times for similar behaviour it is worth pursuing longer-term discipline strategies (see pp. 101f), with collegiate support and parent support where feasible.

DIRECT COMMAND

There's a time to use the universal word 'Oi!' *to gain attention* and issue a command. I was on playground duty recently and saw, from a distance, silly male pushing and shoving get out of hand. A 13-year-old boy started pounding another boy's head; the 'audience' quickly formed.

'Oi!', said loud, sharp, quick. Then drop the voice to an assertive tone with firm direct eye contact. 'Right move away, you over there, you over there,' (use names if you know them). Direct the audience to go. If the students refuse to move, redirect and either get help or (if comfortable and experienced) physically intervene (but see pp. 61-2). I actually had to haul Mike off, direct the others away, hold him for several seconds ('Mike, c'mon, you're uptight, settle down then we'll sort it out). He slammed down on the seat, head on hands and then cried.

Dealing with fighting or bullying is a major issue on which there should be school-wide agreement — a plan. In difficult schools we have either paired playground duty or the red-card system; the card is sent to the office or staffroom to get immediate assistance (see pp. 98-101).

Commands are appropriate for breaches of safety or personal rights. Our tone should be firm, decisive, direct, unmistakable. In unsafe and potentially dangerous situations, keep the voice firm but calm — a sharp tone may exacerbate the danger. Repeat if necessary.

'Put that down now...'
'Leave this classroom and go to...'
'Move away from there immediately.'

THE 4 Ws

As a standard approach for older children, any significant deferred consequence (especially during detention) can benefit from the use of the following questions (on a standard form). It acts as a 'right of reply' and as a precursor to problem-solving.

1. What I did. (Older students, how my behaviour affected the rights of others).
2. What rule my behaviour affected.
3. Why I did it. (My explanation.)
4. What I think I should do to fix 'it'.

A place can be left on the back of the form for teacher comments.

EXIT AND TIME OUT

Where a student has had opportunity to work by the fair rules but his behaviour is significantly affecting the rights of others to learn, feel safe or be treated with dignity, we will have to utilise 'exit' and 'time-out' provisions (see Chapter 5).

Wherever possible, utilise a 'private' choice: 'David, you've chosen not to work by the fair rules, we'll have to ask you to leave and go to...' (whatever the school-wide plan is for time out).

This 'last' step also needs to be carried out with prior planning (school-wide) and as much dignity as we can muster, as some students quickly go 'off' into extremely disruptive behaviour patterns.

DEVELOPING CLASSROOM DISCIPLINE PLANS

Questions to consider

- How does your definition of discipline square with that used in this chapter?
- Several guiding principles of discipline have been outlined. How does your approach relate to these?
- What sort of rules have you established with your students? How were they established? How positively are they stated? How fair (just) are they in your opinion? What part did the students have in forming those rules? Have you discussed rights and responsibilities and consequences (for significant rule-breaking/rights infringement) with your students?
- How conscious are you of having any 'discipline plan' (general or specific)? Are you aware of what you *characteristically* say to students when they are off task or disruptive?
- When students seek to engage you in 'secondary dialogue' (or use 'secondary behaviours') what do you normally do? say?
- How 'decisive' (in the sense used in this chapter) do you regard your *characteristic* discipline/leadership style?
- What areas, in your current practice, can you see yourself modifying (in the short term, in the longer term)?
- What skills or approaches could you/are you, using? How will you go about developing these skills?

Action planning

In developing a more decisive discipline plan you might like to consider the following.

1. How will you deal with the range of classroom disruptions you commonly face?
   - What discipline steps can (will) I take for: Calling out? Talking

out of turn? Butting in? General class noise?

- How can I gain group attention without shouting or yelling (or threatening to keep them all back)?
- How will I deal with seat-wandering and motoric restlessness?
- How will I deal with class clowns? With students who 'fiddle' with pens, books, equipment during instructional time?
- How will I deal with several students who want my attention and help during on-task time?
- How will I deal with task avoiders? Slow workers? Task refusers? Sulkers? The messy, lazy, student?
- How will I deal with quarrelsome students? Those who pick on others? Those who put others down? Who swear in frustration? Who swear at another student (or use racist or sexist language)? Those who damage (or deface) others' work? Displays of unsafe, dangerous behaviour? Teasing and tale-telling?
- How will I deal with the argumentative student? The aggressive student?

2. Rehearse the skills discussed in this chapter, personalise them, ask yourself how you might employ them in your classroom. Even cognitive rehearsal is an effective way of improving one's verbal discipline. You could try saying them to a cassette recorder if your self-esteem can hack it!

3. Consciously address the issue of preventative discipline by re-assessing how classroom organisation (seating, work stations, work procedures, beginning and ending of lessons, mixed ability considerations) affect the discipline dynamic.

4. Consciously plan for discipline transactions at the 'up-front' phase of the lesson (plan to be brief, concentrate on the primary behaviour, demonstrate expectation of compliance). During the 'on-task' phase of the lesson move around, call students aside, keep transactions at the 'least intrusive' level where possible.

5. It can help to keep records of discipline transactions: what specifically occurs, when, with whom, what you did, how effective you believe it was.

6. Establish support processes if you need to exit a student or to develop 'contracts' or special plans with students, if you require any moral or professional support for on-going discipline problems.

5

Follow Up Beyond the Classroom

EXIT AND TIME-OUT PROCEDURES

Persona non grata — where a student's disruptive behaviour *significantly* affects others' rights to feel safe, to learn, to be treated with respect and dignity, we may have to consider the most intrusive step in discipline: time out.

Time out is essentially time away from the group or activity. Time to cool down, be 'removed' from a distracting reinforcement (the group) and rethink. It needs to be seen (and utilised) as a *consequence* rather than a punishment.

Time out would normally occur when a student exhibits:

- Unsafe behaviour (hostile or aggressive behaviour such as stabbing with a pencil, spitting at another student).
- Any continual disruptive behaviour.
- Loud, provocative inter-personal swearing (not frustration swearing — say, dropping something and saying shit!).
- On-going tantrum behaviour that will not settle down after appropriate tactical ignoring and redirection.

Teachers, of course, need to use professional judgement on the degree of rights infringement. It is wise to have a clear school-wide policy for exit from class and time-out provisions.

Like all discipline measures, time out can occur on a least to most intrusive basis. It may be appropriate for some students to take 3–5 minutes COT (cool-off time) in the room. This is quite appropriate at lower primary.

When Sean is getting the 'angries', throwing things about, yelling, spitting on others' work, he is directed (even taken firmly, without shouting) to the COT corner. A few cushions and an egg-timer. He has been taught to sit there, cool down and come back *when* the 'angries' have gone down. He needs (as all children do) to know that angry feelings are not bad, but throwing books around, swearing *at* the teacher, or students, is wrong. The egg-timer gives the student a visble focus, and a sense of personal control; the teacher leaves him with a 'when/then' direction.

With older students a brief spell (5–10 minutes) outside the door *may* be appropriate. Of course, it needs to be stressed that this should only be used with students who are unlikely to clown around outside (I've had students climb up and head-bang windows, gesticulate, etc). If a student is responsibly sitting outside (or standing) it is appropriate for other teachers walking by (even head teachers) not to get involved by discussion. A polite greeting is enough, they don't need the *extra* attention outside unless the student is kicking the door, etc. Some schools will not allow students to be sent outside class as a form of time out. Be sure to clarify school policy on time-out usage.

Sending a student away from class

Directing a student away from your class is a serious step. Imagine how the student feels leaving that open door, over twenty pairs of eyes watching, knowing... To avoid either humiliation or over-servicing possible attention-seeking, it is wise to plan for this 'most intrusive' step.

- Plan what you need to say. Keep it brief, avoid threatening language, focus on the behaviour and the rule (or rights). 'David, I've asked you to settle down, you haven't. You know the class rules. I want you to leave our room now and go to...' If they argue, redirect. Avoid threats, intimidation, or shouting. It will only 'feed' an already tense situation.
- Your students will know (you will have made this point in the establishment phase of the year) that exit and time out is a class consequence for significant disruption.
- Prior to utilising exit provisions it may be possible to distract the student aside in the room (or even just outside the room) either for a *brief* chat or to make the consequence of time out clear to him.

'Dave, you're not normally like this, what's the problem? If you'll calm down, as soon as I've got some time I'll talk it over with you and I'm sure we can work something out, OK?'

This approach is recommended by Glasser (1991). If we make the consequence clear we need to refer briefly to the class rule, the fact that it's been broken, that the student has had time to settle, and this is the final warning. 'If you continue to... I'll have to ask you to leave our class.' (The word 'our' is not accidental.)

- Be sure you know where you can send students, and what you'll do if they refuse to leave (see below).
- Be sure to keep records.
- Be sure to follow up with the student later and with the person you sent the student to.

Remember, when you send a student to a colleague (your co-ordinator, house tutor, head teacher) you are asking for their support 'in the breech' — the emotional moment. You have a right to expect such support. It is unhelpful to just send and forget, or send and expect them to fix it all up and send the student back all 'cured'. You are the one who has an on-going relationship with the student. Utilise senior colleague advice, counsel and support. There may, of course, be mitigating circumstances from home. While this doesn't excuse the student's behaviour in class it can help to put it in perspective and affect outcomes such as counselling and welfare provisions.

If there is a pattern of exit with a student, long-term measures will need to apply. Again this has to be worked out on a school-wide basis.

It is important that the resolution process includes the subject teacher as well as the year co-ordinator. 'Triangular thinking' (de Bono 1986) means fundamentally ensuring that the parties affected by the dispute are involved in its long-term resolution.

Students who refuse to leave the room

Like all effective discipline the possibility of a student refusing to leave (a crisis situation) has to be planned for. If you've ever been in this difficult position you'll know that the heart races, you feel powerless as the student runs around, hides in a cupboard, persists in an extreme form of behaviour. You direct him to leave, the student runs and hides, continues the disruptive behaviour or flatly refuses.

Mrs Snaggs is running a drama lesson. The students are in a half-circle, sitting, listening to her instructions about the lesson. The most difficult student (with a history of hostile behaviour) 'suddenly' grabs the boy next to him and in seconds they're wrestling on the carpet. Swear words, like missiles, are thrown. What will the teacher do?

She commands them to stop. With a final blow, the initiator (who will say the other student 'started it' or 'made me') turns his sulky face away from the teacher. Should she direct him to leave the room? Exit him? This school's policy is that fighting is non-negotiable behaviour. She directs both to leave the room. One reluctantly (muttering under his breath) leaves. The other student refuses to go. What does she do next?

I've worked in may difficult schools where eruptions like this occur. The point was made earlier that for a consequence to be effective it needs to be certain, not necessarily severe. Time out is such a consequence.

Example of a collegiate exit policy
Some years ago, in a very difficult inner-city school, we instituted a collegiate exit/time-out policy to deal with students whose behaviour is extreme, who need to be directed away from a classroom audience, but who refuse to leave for the classroom teacher concerned.

We were well aware that we couldn't make them leave, we were well aware that in the heat of the moment neither teacher nor (often) student wants to 'lose face'. Calling in a third party nearly always made possible a clean 'face-saving' way for all. Remember at this point the student is often into a power-play with the classroom teacher, and the student may 'believe' he is gaining the approval of his peers. (These situations mostly concern male students.)

We devised a simple cue-card system. We called it an exit-card. Each teacher in the school has one. In a situation where an exit-of-student is required the class teacher sends a trusted student to another teacher with the card. The card is a universal cue: 'Help is needed in Room 17.' The green card has the room number on it. The receiving teacher (spatially close as rooms go) leaves her classroom door open, walks across the corridor and calmly directs the refuser to come across to her room. 'Darren, come with me please.' It is said positively, firmly, expectantly.

Of course, there are targeted teachers within each area of the school who can leave their classes *briefly* to walk over and direct a student back to their room. When the student comes across to the supporting teacher's room he normally just sits in that class until the bell goes. A longer-term consequence can be worked out when the student has 'cooled down'.

There are some occasions so serious that we send a card to the office. In this case the card is a red card. It says, basically (in the shorthand of the colour red), a student has jumped out of the window; won't come into class (he's up a tree instead!).

The key to this approach is that:

- It is planned as a whole-school policy.
- It is used as part of a total classroom discipline plan and an exit/ time-out policy.
- Any such exit needs to spell the message that the *consequence* of exit and time out is serious and has to be supported by the whole school. It will have been prefaced by the least intrusive measures mentioned earlier.
- It is not to be used in a cavalier way. Accurate records are kept and remedial behaviour programmes are developed with any student who has been exited in this way.
- It gives support to the affected teacher and the disaffected student, and protects the safety, treatment and learning rights of the rest of the class.

Tammie was a year 9 student (14 years of age) whose background included abuse at home. She came to school with a lot of 'emotional baggage'. Her low tolerance to frustration, heavy-weight sulking, answering back could easily be explained by her background. In terms of a whole-school approach for students, Tammie was receiving counselling, was working with a support teacher on anger-management, but knew she couldn't ever be excused swearing and screaming at teachers (on those bad days), or persistent (repeated) disruption that significantly affected learning or any abuses of the safety rules. She also knew that if any of these occurred one of three teachers (she nominated them) could be sent to direct her from her room. She always went. Uptight; but she went. As part of a *total* policy it had a dramatic and effective impact.

Checklist of questions on exit policy
The questions the individual teacher and the entire staff have to ask are:

1. What sort of behaviours would we expect to 'exit' students from the room for?
2. Will we distinguish (and approve) brief cooling-off-thinking time just outside the room, from the more serious sending of a student away to another area in the school?
3. What will we say to a student when directing her from the room? Have we planned what sorts of things we'll say? (Remember you'll feel quite rattled when such a necessity arises.)

4. What will be our plan 'B' if a student refuses to go?
5. Where will we send her (outside the room, a colleague nearby, the office)?
6. What records will we keep?
7. On what basis will we renegotiate with the student to resolve the issue and allow (later) entry back to class?

It is desirable that these sorts of questions form the basis of a school-wide policy on 'exit' and 'time out'.

DIFFICULT STUDENTS

When working with very difficult students it is essential to have collegiate support. Some of the questions we can ask are:

- Are there any special educational and welfare needs?
- What are the specific disruptive behaviours he engages in, in the class/in the playground?
- In a conflict situation in class how long does it take for the student to settle down (cool down)? Is he/she still acting uptight, sulky, 'blaming' half an hour later?
- How does the student respond to related consequences (pp. 119f)?
- What sort of 'contracts' or 'behaviour agreements' has the student been on?
- Are there teachers in the team (or year level) who have been able to work successfully with this student? If so, what sort of approaches have they taken?
- Have any *school-wide* management plans (especially for conflict situations) been adopted for this student?

FOLLOWING UP STUDENTS BEYOND CLASS

Where the student repeats disruptive behaviour on several occasions it is important for the teacher to follow through with a more concentrated plan. Mention has already been made of the importance of balancing short and long-term approaches (p.61) and the value of out-of-classroom chats away from other students. If a student is repeatedly rude to the teacher in class, however, this attitude problem needs working on after class. The same applies with not having equipment and any *repeated* infractions (chewing gum, seat-leaning, seat wandering, task avoidance, calling out).

CONTRACTS

A 'contract' or behaviour agreement is an approach that seeks to enable student and teacher to clarify:

- who 'owns' what aspects of the problem behaviour;
- why the behaviour is occurring (there may be some mitigating circumstances from home; this can be checked out with senior staff, or the school counsellor);
- how the student should understand *specifically* the effect of his behaviour on others and how it is affecting the rights of others (teacher and student);
- and most importantly what the student can do to change his behaviour so that he can be more successful in class.

As with all significant (extended out-of-classroom) follow up, one needs to observe the ethical constraints of a one-to-one situation. With female students it is advisable that a female colleague be present (abstractedly working) if the initiating teacher is a male.

If a contract or plan or behaviour agreement is going to achieve anything with a difficult student:

- It needs to be seen as a supportive process distinct from normal consequences or punishments. The emphasis is on helping the student to own his behaviour by teacher support, The 'tone' is supportive not punitive. 'How can I help you so your behaviour is successful in class?' If the student sees the contract as another punishment it will not achieve its purpose.
- The student needs to 'own' his behaviour. He needs to agree on the specific wrong behaviours (against rights and rules) and 'own' the change process with teacher support.
- Contracts need to be worked in conjunction with formal counselling and welfare procedures. Many 'difficult' students may already be receiving welfare and counselling but will still need specific contracted guidelines to assist them in behaviour change.
- Contracts will need to be simple, achievable and workable for all. They should also improve, or at least stabilise, the working relationship between student and teacher, and help the student balance his rights and responsibilities.
- If a teacher feels she cannot work on a plan because the relationship is too strained it will be essential to call in the support

of a senior colleague to act as a third party facilitator with both the teacher and student.

Ben has been late to class several times, arrives in class very sulky (he's got the inevitable home problems), has engaged the teacher in significant task avoidance (and sometimes task refusal) and is heavily into 'secondary behaviour' (pp. 25-9).

The class teacher has made an appointment with Ben in classroom time, to 'contract' for behaviour change. Of course, any contract session should be made well after the heat of conflict has gone down. At the time of conflict let him know that you (as well as he) are too angry to discuss the problem now. 'We'll meet later to discuss it.'

'Ben, I want to talk to you about your behaviour in class.' Be specific about the behaviours, even model them to the student. Explain how it affects you and the other students *in terms of basic rights* to teach, to learn, to feel safe, to be treated with respect.

It may also be helpful to say how you think he might be feeling. To express understanding ('I bet you feel..' 'You probably feel annoyed at having to stay back, right?') doesn't mean you agree with the student's behaviour or condone the rule-breaking by the student. You are tuning in at a human level. As Jane Nelson (1981) notes, it may even be appropriate to share times when you've felt (or behaved) similarly ('I can remember once when I was angry with my science teacher...').

Goal disclosure

Rudolf Dreikurs (Dreikurs, Grunwald and Pepper 1982) suggests a process designed to help the student focus on the purpose behind his misbehaviour. This is appropriate if other obvious causes (e.g. family crisis) are not present (see Fig. 3).

In a friendly tone preface the question: 'Ben, you know when you refuse to do the work in class' (the teacher can, tongue in cheek, model the behaviour) and then ask 'Do you know why you do that?' Most students will not answer. We can proceed with, 'I'd like to tell you what I think. Could it be that you are trying to show me I *can't make you* do the work? I *can't make you* stay in your seat? You know when you come into class and slam the door, and throw yourself into your seat... could it be you want us all *to notice you*?' Remember the point of this exchange is not to force the student into a face-losing state or make him feel small. It is a way of helping the student to see that you see, too, what his purpose might be. 'Could it be you butt in a lot (ten times the other morning) because you want me to notice you a lot? Or because

Attention-seeking

- You want to keep me busy with you?

- You want me to notice you more?

- You want to keep the group busy with you?

Power struggle

- You want to be the boss? You want to be in charge?

- You want to show me that you can do what you want?
  You want to show me that I can't stop you?

- You want to do what you want when you want? You want to
  show me that 'no one' can stop you?

Revenge seeking

- You want to punish me?

- You want to show me how it feels?

- You want to make me suffer?

- You want to hurt me and the students in the class?

Inadequacy

- You feel you can't do anything?

- You are afraid to fail?

- You feel like you don't know the answer and don't want people
  to know?

- You want me to stop asking you to do it?

Fig. 3. Goal disclosures
(Adapted from Driekurs, Grunwald and Pepper, 1982)

you want the other students to notice you a lot?'

Most students will not say 'yes' or 'no' to this but will look up, away, and back; even with a smile sometimes. This is what Dreikurs calls a 'recognition reflex'. I normally respond with 'I thought that's why you did 'x' 'y' 'z'.' If they say 'no!', simply say, 'Well, I thought that's why you did it. Can *you* explain why you do...?'

The next step is to agree in part with their goal. 'Well, Ben I can't *make* you do...' 'I can't *stop* you being angry.' 'I can't *simply stop* you calling out, or butting in.' 'What I need is your help to make a plan, OK?'

The agreed plan

If they agree, move along with a plan that can help them work by the fair rules and still get recognition. One student who was regularly butting in and talkative made a plan with his teacher to keep a record of when he felt he butted in and compare it with the teacher's record. Both had a small 'catch me' card. This helped the student to refocus his behaviour and still receive teacher attention.

With Ben's anger episodes the teacher explained that he, i.e. the teacher, hadn't handled them well by at times over-reacting. This admission surprised Ben, (I've noticed a number of students show surprise at a teacher's honesty and frank admission, for example, when I've told students that I can't *make* them do things).

'Ben, are you aware of what 'makes' you uptight or angry in class?' 'You know, when I get angry I feel... My shoulders tense... Are you aware of what happens to you when you get angry? Try this week to catch yourself when you get angry and see what happens to your body, OK? Next time we meet we can compare notes.' This puts some responsibility back on the student. Or we could give him a simple little anger management plan. 'When you get really uptight, stop, count back from 10, slowly relax your shoulders, arms, hands, and refocus on your plan. Say to yourself, 'OK, I feel angry, but I can deal with it when I....' If you're really uptight I won't be upset if you quietly leave the class and signal with your hand that you're leaving.' I'd rather have a really uptight student leave the class for a few minutes, walk around outside, have a drink and come back, than 'explode' in class. (This plan would need to be checked by a senior staff member.) This is a simple 'when, then' plan. Write it down on a small card which they can keep in their diary.

- Plans can be expressed in writing (or in pictorial form for younger students), outlining behaviours they need to stop, behaviours they need to start, equipment they need to remember to bring to class, or arrival times. It is best to concentrate on a few behaviours at a time and to express them specifically and simply.

- Remember to encourage effort. If the student has a bad day it doesn't invalidate the plan; after normal time out and other consequences, he can (and should be encouraged to) come back into the contract arrangement. Rewards may be appropriate with a contract plan but discuss this with your supervisor.
- Wean the student off the 'plan' as his behaviour improves.

Remember, you may not see a complete cessation of troublesome behaviour. If there is a reduction in *frequency* and *intensity* that will be success and will probably enable normal classroom disciplinary procedures to operate once again.

CONTRACT SUPERVISION

At the secondary level, if several teachers are reporting problems with an individual student and each are trying, and doing, different things, it can be more productive to appoint a 'contract supervisor'. The contract supervisor would normally be the year co-ordinator. It is important that the supervisor be someone able to communicate well, and work effectively, with students. He or she will work with the student on a plan that will be communicated back to all subject teachers. The contract supervisor will work with the student to identify and own the problem behaviours, encourage the student to make a plan, with the supervisor's support, and 'practise' the elements of the plan. The supervisor will liaise with subject teachers and the student on a daily basis if necessary.

Essentially the plan will be a simple restructuring of the student's responsibilities within the classroom (and school) rules. If a plan can be worked out it will be important that each subject teacher support the plan by using non-confrontational discipline and encouragement. In other words, the philosophical direction of the contract is as important as the stated words.

Built into the plan will be a clear exit policy for difficult to manage students (pp. 96-7). In some cases it will be appropriate for co-ordinators to call a meeting of the subject teachers who work with the student to outline the joint contract plan.

If the student refuses to co-operate with a contract supervisor, 'I'm not making any plan!!', the supervisor will outline the consequences, to the student, for *continuing* in these (be specific) behaviours. After all, we can't make the student co-operate though many will if the approach is supportive rather than confrontational.

CONTRACTING WITH LOWER PRIMARY STUDENTS

At the primary level it can be helpful to run contracting sessions with difficult students in out-of-class time. This will mean another teacher covering your class. As there are normally less than 5 per cent of such students in a school (in terms of frequency and intensity of disruptive behaviour) a rota for peer support for those teachers wishing to pursue a contract approach ought to be able to be worked out.

To be successful with lower and middle primary students, emphasis should be on the following:

- Identify with the student the specific off-task behaviours. The teacher can (tongue-in-cheek) model those behaviours.
- Explain how it upsets the teacher and students alike. If you can draw simple cartoons or have some drawn for you, this can add to the concreteness of your explanation.
- Show them a simple plan to help them in class. The plan can be drawn on a card. 'This plan is to help you remember what to do in class.'
- *Model* the target behaviour to the student. Keep it simple and concentrate on one or two behaviours. 'Stay in your seat until the egg-timer is finished, then come over to show me your work. I'll take you back and you start again.' The use of an egg-timer can help physically restless students to refocus.
- Get the student to demonstrate that he can do his plan. Role-play it together. Give him feedback as he practises his plan with you. Ask him questions, check he understands. Explain how he can use it in class, perhaps with a copy of the plan (in a plastic folder) on his table.
- Encourage him when he keeps to his plan. If you use a reward schedule trade in 20 ticks for a special sticker or free activity.

6

Rights, Responsibilities, Rules and Consequences

'I mete and dole unequal laws unto a savage race that know and feed me not.'

Alfred Lord Tennyson

THE ESTABLISHMENT PHASE OF THE YEAR

Some teachers call it the 'honeymoon period', I call it the establishment phase. Supply teachers go through it with each class they take; regular teachers go through it in the first few weeks. The students are checking the teacher out: Has she got a sense of humour? How strict is she? What will the lessons be like? Can we sit where we want? What's her discipline like? Her marking? Does she follow things up? The students, as a group, are expecting clarification of *how* you will lead them. They are ready for you to state your expectations and reveal your 'style' of leadership.

Doyle (1986, pp. 410,411) notes wide research showing that all teachers introduced some rules and procedures on their first few days. Effective teachers, however, integrated rules and procedures into a workable system. The rules and procedures were concrete, explicit, functional and clearly explained. Cues, signals, and class procedures were rehearsed. In contrast, less effective managers failed to anticipate the need for rules and procedures covering important aspects of class operation or tended to have vague and unenforceable rules. Effective managers were rated higher on clarity of directions and information, stating desired behaviours more frequently, presenting clear expectations for work standards, *responding consistently to appropriate and inappropriate behaviour*, stopping disruptive behaviour sooner and using rules and procedures more frequently to deal with disruptive behaviour. According to Doyle, the amount of disruptive behaviour did not differ significantly between 'less' and 'more' effective managers during the first week of school. There was in the second and third weeks, for ineffective teachers, an increase in the areas of 'call-outs', 'talking in class' and 'movement around the room'. Successful managers anticipated problems and how to deal with them.

The first week or so is an important time to make clear to your students how you expect this class to work. The way we establish an understanding of the four Rs — what their Rights are, the Responsibilities that go with those rights, and the fair Rules that protect rights and challenge responsibility, and classroom Routines — determines the basis of our discipline and management. The routines we establish for entering and leaving classrooms, bell times, getting to class on time (including the teacher!), work distribution and retrieval, clarifying work/task requirements, seating plans, monitor systems... all establish the smooth running of a class. All this is *preventative* management.

CLASSROOM RIGHTS

The language of rights is now a fixture in students' understanding and language. 'I've got my rights!' is an oft-heard statement. Our job as teacher-leaders is to clarify that a right is not inviolable. A right is an expectation of how things *ought* to be when we're acting, and others are acting, responsibly. As such, rights can be removed'. If students' behaviour is *significantly* disruptive, they need to know that they may have to work away from others or in some cases leave the room until they have 'cooled off' and thought about working by the fair rules.

Rights come from what we *value*. A right, therefore, is not arbitrary. It explains the issues and behaviours we value, that we believe are right and proper. For example, we believe people ought to be treated with respect regardless of ethnic origin, colour, gender, religion, ability, disability. We express this as a *treatment* right (as does the United Nations).

The three fundamental rights in a classroom (indeed in school generally) are:

- The right to feel safe
- The right to be treated with respect
- The right to learn (within one's ability range)

Rights such as the right of reply, the right to an opinion, the right to have one's property and person respected can all be subsumed under the rights noted above.

TEACH RIGHTS WITH RESPONSIBILITIES

Appropriate to age, teachers can *teach* students about rights and responsibilities. Allowing appropriate discussion by students can enhance the relationship aspects of rights (rather than listing a set of student or teacher demands). Teacher modelling will also convey how fundamental rights are valued: if a teacher ignores racist language, or 'put-downs' used interpersonally, or says that students have a right to co-operate and have their say but stifles appropriate student contribution, the teacher has clearly communicated there is little meaning in these rights.

- If you have a *right to your say*, you have a responsibility to listen when others speak, to take your turn, and not 'put others down'.
- If you have a *right to have your property respected*, you have a responsibility to respect others' property (if you want to borrow, ask first then put it back later).
- If you want to be *treated with respect*, treat others with respect (teachers too!).

Operational definitions of respect

You don't need to like someone (necessarily) to respect them. I don't believe one can be an effective teacher without liking young people, in the general sense; there will, however, be some students we will not like but we will need to respect them professionally. **Respect is an action**, something we can do whether we like or dislike the other person. This social axiom needs to be modelled by the teacher:

- Address the behaviour rather than attacking the person.
- Be aware of body language: avoid pointing, slamming hands on desks, getting spatially close in a conflict situation.
- Avoiding holding grudges.
- Remember the basics like first names, 'please', 'thanks', 'excuse me', 'good morning'.
- Re-establish working relationships after discipline incidents.

Our students need to be taught that respect is shown in basics like saying 'please' and 'thanks'; asking if you want to borrow; saying 'excuse me' if you want to pass through or someone is in your way; returning borrowed items; using first names; using language that helps people feel good about themselves (no put-downs, racist or sexist language, no swearing).

RULES: BALANCING RIGHTS AND RESPONSIBILITIES

Rules, or classroom agreements, are needed to protect fundamental rights and outline what is appropriate social behaviour: what is expected, what is safe, what is fair (reasonable) and what the limits are. They are the basis for all forms of discipline (classroom, corridor, playground, excursion) in that they define the protective limits to rights and invoke the responsibilities inherent in those rights.

While we can't simply legislate to change attitude and behaviour we can set an agreed context through discussion and common expectations about what ought to be. The central message is 'you own your own behaviour' and respect mutual rights.

I've been in many classrooms, working with teachers, who have said 'The students know the rules, we don't need to go over them again this year.' The point is the students need to know with you *this* year, what the expectations are. And remember, students 'forget'. Classrooms without known rules, agreements or procedures can be very noisy, unstable places. I've sat in class discussions where only the loudest get a say, when several students compete for question time. At the beginning of the year it will be important to determine, with your students, appropriate communication rules to minimise unnecessary disruption.

Because the school is a community and its members come from varying backgrounds, and varying value positions, the school community needs to agree that some things are fundamentally right about the way we relate to and work at school. Teachers and students (fundamentally) have the same rights, though different responsibilities.

- **Teachers** at the school are entitled to expect the right to teach without harassment and unwarranted disruption. They also have the responsibility to prepare well for lessons, give reliable and supportive feedback to students, cater for mixed abilities within the classes and treat students with dignity and respect. This last point does not deny the need to discipline with assertion where rights to teach, learn and feel safe are being infringed.

The fundamental **rights in a classroom** (these overlap into the wider school environment) would include:

- A treatment right: the right to be treated equally regardless of religious, cultural, ethnic, sexual or physical differences. It includes an expectation of the right to be treated fairly and with dignity.

- A communication right: the right to have one's say, share ideas, express oneself, ask questions.
- A safety right: the right to feel safe at school; to feel free from intimidation in class or out of class; to be safe and secure in person and property.
- A right to learn: the right to learn without interference, within one's ability, in a reasonable working environment and with appropriate teacher assistance.
- A movement right: a right to safe movement about the class and school at certain times in a reasonable manner.
- A right of reply: the right to tell your side of the story, a right to rational settlement of problems.

Many children have a basic sense of right or wrong (in a culturally derived sense); part of our job is clarifying rights and values — what the right thing means here in this class, this school.

Rules are closely related to rights and will need to cover the topics listed above. A rule for the way we treat one another. A rule for safety, for communication, for interpersonal treatment, for movement, for learning time, for settling problems.

Shaping the rules

For a rule to be serviceable it needs to be clear, fair and 'owned' by the students, have a positive balance where possible, and be enforced and enforceable.

Clear

'Hands up in class' is not clear. Many students put their hand up yet call out or click fingers at the same time. 'Hands up without calling out' is clearer. 'Be kind' or 'Be nice' is not as clear as a respect rule that outlines *what* actions of respect are important in class (what 'niceness' means operationally).

Positive in intent

Where possible outline the positive aspect of the rule as well as the negative. '*Walk quietly in class* (don't run)'. '*Hands up* (without calling out!)'. '*Keep your hands and feet to yourself* (this means no pushing, pulling, hitting.)' Use *positive* language that helps people to feel good about themselves and others (this means no racist language, no put-downs or sexist language or swearing).

Fair

A rule needs to be seen as fair both in its application and in its enforcement. One way to develop a sense of fairness is to enable the students to 'own' the rules by classroom discussion in the establishment phase of the year.

'Owning' the rules

At lower primary the teacher can use picture-card rules and discuss why we have rules at home, on the sports field, in our games: What games do you play? What are the rules for those games? Why do we have rules? Who makes the rules? (at home? at school? in games?) What happens when rules are broken? Why? Picture-card rules illustrate an aspect of the rule, say, our talking rule, by showing students with hands up (and mouths closed) and another picture of students with 'quiet talk bubbles' working at their desks. The manners rule is portrayed in picture form as several students speaking with positive manners ('please', 'ta', 'thanks', 'can I borrow?', 'excuse me').

These picture-rules are displayed on a wall under the heading: 'Our classroom rules.' In the establishment phase the lower primary teacher will use these cards as discussion aids: 'Who can tell what's happening on this card?' Paul calls out, 'Anyway Miss they got their hands up.' The teacher chooses to ignore Paul. It's a *tactical* move (she doesn't dislike Paul). Richard puts his hand up as do several others — without calling. 'Yes Richard.' The teacher is casually eye-scanning the room and as she answers Richard's question she notices Paul copy; he puts his hand up without calling out. 'Yes Paul, I see your hand up. Thanks for waiting.' The teacher, by her behaviour, is both explaining and reinforcing the rule. She will refer to her rules regularly after she has taught them. They form the basis for her discipline plan.

It can be helpful to either:

1. Discuss basic rules or classroom agreements with the class to gain their understanding or agreement, *or*
2. Invite them to brainstorm with you around these six key areas:
   - the way we treat one another in class,
   - the way we learn here,
   - how we can feel (and be) safe in our class,
   - how problems (especially interpersonal problems) are settled in class,
   - how we communicate with one another in class (this interfaces with the respect and learning rule),

- how we care for our classroom environment (this includes one another's property).

At middle and upper primary level we can let the students work in a group activity where they can write up the rules using a balance of positive/negatives. A classroom meeting is also an effective way to establish class agreements if you are comfortable with the group (see p. 133).

Another, longer-term, method (primary level)

1. Begin by asking the students about rules used on the road, at home, in school, in sport, etc. and *why* they exist. Students could work in small groups for ten minutes and then report back to the rest of the class. Ideas could then be noted and used for a class discussion.
2. Tell the students you would like to establish rules for the class and want them to participate in making the class rules. Students can work in small groups listing their suggestions about 'good'; rules that will help us learn and get on well together and help us to feel safe in class.
3. Collect their ideas and at home that night form these into five or six rules.
4. The next day show the students the rules you've worked out from their suggestions. Give examples from their lists and show where they have been included.
5. Explain that five or six rules rather than lots of rules are easier for us to learn, remember and work by. Students can write up these rules on large cards (one per group) and display them in the room.
6. Finally, discuss with the class the accountability side of the rules. If a student infringes other people's rights (by breaking the rules) then there will be consequences. These are behavioural *outcomes* that fit the rule-breaking behaviour. For example, a consequence of a student wasting time during a lesson would be that the student completes the work missed in his or her own time, or if a student damages someone else's property he or she will replace it and so on.

   One way of doing this is to ask the students, working in small groups, to decide what consequence ought to apply for certain behaviours. Often they will be quite severe and the teacher will need to ask, 'Well, how does that consequence help to fix that behaviour?' so that students reach an understanding of a consequence which fits the rule-breaking behaviour.

THE LANGUAGE OF RULES

Framing the language of rules is never easy. Some teachers prefer a bold heading with several sub-points, as in the following suggested guidelines:

Communication
- Hands up without calling out.
- Respectful language with others (no put downs or racist or sexist language).
- Listen when others speak and one at a time.
- Hands up without calling out if you need teacher help. (This varies according to subject area.)
- Face the front and listen during teaching time. Hands up (or one at a time) in class discussion.

Learning
- Quiet working noise at your tables (or desks).
- Hands up (without calling out) if you need my help; or ask three before you ask me.
- Take care to consider your working space, and others.

Manners
- Please, thanks, excuse me. Watch others 'personal space'.
- Respectful language with each other (no poking fun or put downs allowed).
- Ask if you want to borrow another's property. Give it back that lesson.

Safety
- Take care, use common sense (accidents can happen quickly, easily).
- Use equipment properly. (In science classes, physical education, art, textiles, machine shop there will be *specific* safety rules.)
- If we use equipment in an unsafe way we will not be allowed to use it until we agree to use it safely and correctly.

Movement
Varies again according to subject area and age. The rule should specify reasonable movement, safe movement that doesn't interfere with others' rights. For example to go to the toilet during instructional time

would (normally speaking) be unacceptable. At Reception and Year 1, we have to ask do we want the students to line up and if so, how? Do they sit on the mat when they come in? For Year 8 woodwork, do they sit on the work benches straight away?

Let students know that they are responsible for their own behaviour. Make it clear that if they make it difficult for others to learn, to feel safe, to be treated with respect, they will be asked to work away, or sit away, from others; they may be asked to 'fix up things' after class (deferred consequences), they may be asked to leave the class for time out.

Prior to any of these consequences you will have used least intrusive measures.

Care for our room
- Put things back in their proper place (cupboards, work stations, tool areas, etc. should be clearly labelled). This includes chairs under tables.
- All litter in the bin. (Remind prior to the end of each lesson in the establishment phase).
- Care for others' property.

Problem-fixing
If we've got a problem we use the problem-fixing rule.

- If we can't agree we take cool-off time (work away or sit away till we've cooled down).
- We go through the four Ws:
  What's the problem between us?
  Why do I/you think it happened?
  What rule (or right) was affected? (This for older students.)
  What can I do to fix things?
  This can be used in written form (the 4W form) by the students themselves later in the lesson if feasible, or with teacher assistance working through each question. The key is to establish a conflict-resolution procedure. Fighting or arguing is unacceptable in class. Teach students the value of cool-off time — even adults find it difficult to fix problems when they are uptight, really anxious or angry.
- Classroom meetings will be held to solve problems. You can raise your concerns with the whole class if you want. (Some teachers utilise classroom meetings as a problem-solving forum.)

PUBLISHING THE RULES

Primary level

At primary level it can be helpful to publish the rules in the first week. Large cards (even laminated), with illustrations, on a wall as a focus for 'the way our classroom works'. At middle-school I've had students 'publish' them and monitors put them up on a weekly basis (it can help to laminate the final product).

At primary level class teachers can send a class note home to parents outlining the fair rules and consequences with brief, simple, discussion on classroom discipline and positive consequences. We'll need to check it with our head teacher first. The tone will be positive with an explanation that discipline is essentially guidance; the way we help our students to be responsible and co-operate. Students can illustrate the fair rules (and consequences) in a class booklet to accompany the letter.

Parent contact and support

A key feature of any management process is to give feedback to, and seek appropriate assistance of, the parents. Parents have a right to be informed about the welfare and behaviour of their children and their support can be beneficial — save in those situations where the child comes from an 'at-risk' home environment. Before notifying parents, however, most children (especially at adolescent level) appreciate a chance to resolve their school-based behaviour problems. In any case, discussion with a senior colleague before a parent conference is called is appropriate, and use discretion when describing a child's behaviour in a note home or in a child's school diary.

Secondary level

Another way of setting out rules at the secondary level (a more formal approach) is to outline your expectations in a class letter on the first day to be included in their subject book/folder.

Introduce yourself: 'Hi: I'm your new teacher (name). We'll have a great time this year....' Then set out work and behaviour expectations. 'This is what I'll be expecting of you...' and 'This is what you can expect of me....'

Set out the expectations specifically, positively, and not too many. Set out work requirements *and* behaviour requirements:

'I'll expect you to listen when I'm speaking and the same with each other.'

'I'll expect you to bring the necessary equipment to class.'

'Use your class time to the best of your ability.'

'Give the work your "best shot". I'll help as much as I can even after class where possible. Never be frightened of asking for my help.'

'I'll give you regular feedback on your work and how you're doing.'

One of my colleagues had written on his class letter: 'I'll sometimes have "bad" days like you. When we have bad days let's say so, give ourselves some cool-off time and then fix up where we've gone wrong. OK?'

A more 'open' variation of this theme is to use the 1,3,6 method. Get them to write down their personal expectations of you as a teacher (what kind of teacher? what do you expect of me?). After ten minutes they get together in groups of three to share and put their expectations on one list. They join into a group of six to form a master list. The teacher brainstorms with the class from the lists.

The next step is to repeat the process by asking, 'What can I (ought I) to expect from you as my students?'

The final step is to pursue rights, responsibilities and rules. This approach generally needs two sessions to complete satisfactorily but can be quite effective as a year starter.

SCHOOL-WIDE RULES

School-wide rules are normally non-negotiable although it can be helpful to have a school-wide review every few years involving staff and students.

School-wide rules infringe on class rules; for example, uniform, eating in school buildings, arrival-in-class times, sexual harassment, verbal harassment and racism, violent behaviour, damage to school property.

With regard to uniform a whole-school policy is needed on what are infringements and how they should be addressed. Some teachers have a petty, almost martinet stance, on earrings, make up, dress code. Most uniform issues can be dealt with during class time (not up front in a big public way) or at the end of class by a reminder. If there's a pattern of infringement it can be referred to after-class sessions to find out if there are any other long-term reasons why the student can't observe policy.

ROUTINES

During the establishment phase of the year it is important to clarify the common phases of classroom life: entry, settling down routines (including taking the register), the instructional or 'lesson' time, the on-task activity, pack up time and exit.

Every teacher in every method area needs to clarify how these phases work for them. The phases can be subsumed into two broad areas: 'up-front' and 'on-task' time.

Up front

Normally speaking, up-front time requires the student to be attentive to the teacher's directions. Discipline during this phase needs good eye-scanning, general and specific directions (and rule reminders) and the ability to keep the 'lesson flow' without over-dwelling on any specific incident. It is important to keep directions and reminders brief and then resume the flow. The use of humour and distractions and diversions are very effective in front of an 'audience'. Questions, though, as a form of discipline would not normally be used because of time. It exposes the teacher to too much 'secondary behaviour' to be asking a direct question about behaviour in front of so large a group (e.g. 'What do you want to go to the toilet now for?!').

- In a lively discussion there may be a bit of distracting 'side' chatter. If this is not (unnecessarily) upsetting the ebb and flow it can easily be tactically ignored.
- If calling out occurs as a result of exuberance, a simple preventative measure can be the reminder. 'OK, before I ask any questions I know some of you will be bursting to share the answers. Remember, give each other a fair go, it'll be one at a time and hands up without calling out, OK. Let's go for it.' The teacher uses a balance of rule reminder, brief (simple) directions, distraction and diversion and encouragement.

It is important when up-front to establish a sense of 'presence' and 'expectation of compliance' with your directions and class rules, expectations, routines and agreements. When up-front you need their *group* attention and this is a skill worth developing. It is advisable not to shout and yell in order to establish this (or hit the blackboard or slam the ruler down). Once we habituate a loud pattern, students get used to it and it leaves little manouvreablity.

At primary level (Years 1 to 3), a conditional reinforcer can also be used. *While* giving a general direction to the class a bell is rung. This associates the noise with the direction. After several directions plus bell delivery try it without the bell. You may need to go back to the paired association from time to time but it is an effective, consistent routine for gaining attention. When I taught in primary schools I used a guitar chord as a 'conditional reinforcer' to establish group attention time.

On-task

During 'on-task' time the teacher can (and where preferable should) move around the classroom or group, to remind, check, encourage, direct, redirect. Student attention now (theoretically) is focused on the task or activity. Working noise is allowed and a range of movement by students may be tolerated depending on subject area. Discipline during this time can be more private, one to one. We can use the widest range of discipline repertoire during on-task time. We can quietly move over to distract and divert or use casual statements and questions. The classroom is a *dynamic* setting and teachers will have to divide their attention between a number of needs and demands. At any one point the teacher will be tactically ignoring one situation, humorously defusing yet another, using simple directions or reminding about class rules. With one or two students it may be necessary to make consequences for continued disruption clear. At any stage of the lesson it will be important to target disrupting students carefully. If you're not sure who is actually disrupting it's better to give a general direction or reminder in that part of the room, rather than run the risk of 'mistargetting'.

CONSEQUENCES

The Years 4s were sitting on the carpet area during up-front instructional time. Luke was abstractedly peeling the Formica edge off the teacher's desk. I directed him very briefly (with a hand motion to stop and move away, 'Facing this way Luke'). He'd pulled off a fair section. Should there be a consequence? If so what? Lines? Detention? I directed him to stay back at recess.

T   Luke, I saw you pull off this (I pointed) remember?
S   But Max did, too, the other day!
T   I saw you peel off all this today. What will you do to fix it? ([I didn't yell or shout, just asked and expected.]
S   I could put some Prittstick on it?
T   Do you think Prittstick would hold it on? Prittstick is glue for paper.

S   The other white glue? [He meant PVA]
T   OK Luke, get a brush and some glue. It might be a good idea to
         stick some tape on it to hold it down.

It took him five minutes or so to fix it. The consequence was related,
reasonable and designed to teach responsibility.

Natural consequences

From an early age children are aware of, and learn from, cause and
effect. There is a *relationship* between not brushing your teeth and the
dentist. Fall over the wrong way and often you get hurt (we all have
childhood memories of that). If you don't eat you get hungry. If you
never smile it's doubtful if you'll get many friends. Stand in the sun too
long... Leave your toys out in the rain and....

Teachers (and parents) can build on this natural relationship
('If...then') as a framework for social consequences for *behaviour*.
Based on a rights-responsibility approach and known (fair) rules,
teachers can teach and develop an environment where children make
choices that determine outcomes in positive or negative ways.

Dreikurs (Dreikurs, Grunwald and Pepper, 1982) described this
approach as 'logical' consequences where the intervention of the adult
establishes the connection between behaviour and outcome. It is
important though, to teach children what we *mean* by consequences.

Establishing consequences

As part of a rights-responsibility focus we are seeking to teach children
that they are responsible (under our guidance) and accountable for
how they behave. In the context of natural justice children can learn
from the kind of consequences teachers apply. In fact, consequences
are a more powerful 'teacher' than a long-winded nagging. 'How-
many-times-have-I-told-you...!'

In the 'establishment phase' of the year, teachers will discuss the
question, 'What should happen when, if...'

- if a student swears in class?
- if a student calls out several times?
- if a student hits another student in class?
- if students argue... snatch equipment... don't do their work...
  won't clean up...?

Of course, some consequences in a school cannot be negotiated (discussed, yes), for example, smoking, bullying and fighting, sexual harassment. On major issues affecting fundamental treatment and safety rights, schools need to set clear consequences but also discuss these with students (via the student representative council) and publish them in the school policy.

Related consequences

If a student scribbles on another's work, merely giving detention is not a logical consequence — it is an empty punishment. Rewriting the work for that student, later when the initial conflict has gone down, or doing some positive act for that student, is a *related* consequence.

When there is clear violation of known rules, teachers will bring into effect an 'if...then' dynamic.

- If you choose not to work within the class working-noise rule, you will be expected to work separately, or sit away.
- If you use any equipment unsafely you may have to work without it, or do something else.
- If you do messy, sloppy work, you will be given the chance to re-do or re-work it.
- If you damage equipment, you replace, correct, or work to repay (see later).
- If you make it difficult for others to feel safe — time-out.

Children see more justice in this than *unrelated* punishment like lines, copying out of dictionaries, picking up rubbish (unless of course picking up rubbish is related to dropping it or creating a mess), sitting for thirty minutes in detention, writing out the school rules, keeping the whole class back for the misdemeanours of a few, or even several. If a student is to write out anything it is better he write *about* his behaviour (see the 4W form) and how he thinks he might change it.

Discussion of consequences

Classroom meetings are a useful way of enabling a class to explore fair, related consequences (see p. 133). Not all teachers are comfortable with this approach and some may prefer designing a range of consequences for typical disruptive behaviours and inviting student feedback and discussion.

Teachers can also benefit from staff discussions on developing class-based and school-wide consequences rather than having to often think them up 'on the spot' as it were. This is essential for less serious issues like lateness, eating in class, uniform misdemeanours, playing ball in no-ball areas, and so on. These behaviours can often be dealt with by positive correction rather than consequences such as detention.

Timing of consequences
Logical consequences are best applied when the initial heat has died down. This could be in class time or (often) after class. For example, if a child has sworn at another (or used racist/sexist language) it will be difficult to get an apology at *that* point.

T   Right — apologise now!
S   No!! Why should I, yer didn't hear what she said did yer?! No, you're always on the girls' side!!
T   Don't tell me whose side I'm on — I told you to apologise and I meant it!
S   Can't make me!!
T   Yes I can!
S   No you can't...!

Deferred consequences need to be applied, rather than inflame an already tense situation. If necessary, direct the student to leave (p. 96) to allow cool-off time, and direct both to stay back later and work out the consequences.

Kirstie was chewing up paper in art and lobbed several 'spit balls' on to the opposite bench. The teacher directed her to stop, and clean it up. 'It's not just me you know!' The teacher redirected and avoided a stand-up row. 'If you choose not to clean it up now, you'll have to stay back at recess.' Kirstie had a last word (replete with pout — got to have that pout Kirstie!) 'Don't care!' The teacher walked off leaving Kirstie to the consequences of her 'choice'.

At recess, Kirstie stood by the door. If she had bolted (it happens) the teacher could have followed it up with support from senior staff — later.

T   Kirstie, I want you to clean up the mess now, thanks — I gave you a choice before.
S   It's not all mine!
T   If anybody else was involved let me know and I can follow it up. I want you to clean up the mess I saw you make. [The teacher gestured to the cleaning materials and moved away (within the room) to avoid any further confrontation and allow 'take-up time'.]

Muttering a few low-grade expletives, Kirstie grumpily completed the task. Her audience had gone now. 'OK I cleaned the bloody mess up.' The teacher ignored the secondary behaviours and said 'Thanks Kirstie see you next week.' The teacher did not *add* to the consequence a lecture on the evils of spit-balling — that's unnecessary. When she met Kirstie in the playground she said 'Hi'. The teacher didn't hold any grudges. Next week Kirstie couldn't have been nicer.

Consequences are not punishment

If consequences are applied as retribution (sarcasm, 'serves you right!!', 'I'm sick and tired of your stupid behaviour — well you can suffer now!!!') they will backfire, being seen only as punishment. *Intentional* suffering is not a necessary feature of consequences. Rather we are seeking to stress the responsibility side of a right and the accountability side of a rule (Rogers 1991a).

I often find it useful (after the initial heat) to ask the student how he or she thinks they can fix 'this'. 'What will you do...?' If their solution is unrelated ('I'll do three thousand lines') I ask, 'How will that help you to fix the scratch on the desk? Fix the book you tore? The glue you spilt when you pushed Sean's work off his desk? Fix the scribbling on Anna's book? Catch up on your work because of time-wasting? Fix the broken window?'

Writing apologies, or writing about their behaviour, is also an appropriate consequence. It is important to discuss with the student the concept of 'choice'. You chose this situation:

- *How* can you fix it?
- *What* can you do?
- *Which* of these solutions is best?
- *How* will you do it?
- *How* can I help?

Of course, some consequences are set already by school policy. Others will need to be worked out on a case-by-case situation.

With bullies a useful short-term consequence is to deprive them of social play for a period of time. They have their play times alone — with a minder. While the class is inside, he is outside. While the class is outside at play, he is inside. He'll 'spit chips' but the message (applied firmly but not aggressively, after all that's what we're trying to minimise!) is, 'We cannot let you hurt others, it is wrong and against *our* rule.' 'If you keep hurting others, you'll have to play alone.' 'We can help you play without hurting.' With this consequence we need the active, agreed, support of our peers to share the load. Such students often need an on-going behaviour programme as well as a short-term consequence such as play deprivation.

Of course, teachers will need to distinguish between accidents and mistakes and deliberate flouting of class (or school) rules. Teachers will also have to discuss mitigation for those students with significant emotional trauma from home (or 'at-risk' situations). In these cases check with senior staff before applying consequences beyond normal class-related ones such as working away from others or time-out when safety or treatment rights are significantly affected.

Time-trade consequences
When Nathan damaged the computer keyboard in a fit of pique, we didn't ring Mum (Mum didn't damage it – anyway, he's got quite a disturbed home life), we asked him when he'd cooled down how he would pay to fix it. 'Got no money.' 'OK, Nathan, what can you do here to help pay for what you've broken?' He finally agreed, through discussion with his Year tutor, to do some jobs around the school in his own time and to lose out on a day excursion (the money for that could also help). We call this sort of consequence a 'time-trade' consequence.

One example of the creative use of related consequences for a broken window occurred when the teacher asked the culprits how they could repay. They made soft toys (with the support of the art teacher), sold them and used the proceeds!

A time-trade consequence can be used where the student has damaged school property. When the student has cooled off after a 'damage' incident he and the teacher will work out a time-trade. This is normally a series of jobs around the school, in his own time (cleaning windows, litter clean-up, book-repairing, artroom clean up, playground clean up, gardening).

- Invite their suggestion for 'trade' (trade your time to pay for...)
- Draw up the list of jobs that will form the 'contract'.
- Organise supervision and feedback.

Summary
Related consequences acknowledge and emphasise:

- The reality of the situation rather than just 'power', 'punishment' and authoritarianism.

- A relationship between the disruptive behaviour and the outcome applied.
- A maintaining of respect by separating the 'deed' from the 'doer'.
- 'Choice' within a *known* rights, responsibilities and rules context.
- That students need to experience the consequences of their own behaviour (the 'choosing' idea) rather than just the imposition of outside power.
- Teaching a child about internal control rather than just wanting to control the child.
- The students should see the relevance of the consequence and have the opportunity to try again rather than have their past deeds held against them.

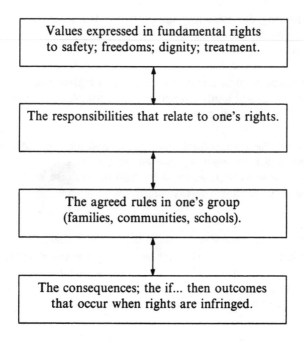

Fig. 4. Balancing freedoms and responsibilities

7

Special Situations for Discipline and Management

THE NOISY CLASS

Most teachers will tolerate 'reasonable' working noise, though the degree varies somewhat. Where that noise level is interfering with teaching and learning it has to be addressed as a discipline and management issue.

- Chattering or distracting talking while the teacher is teaching interferes with the teacher's right to teach, a student's right to learn, and anyway it's lousy manners.

Noise level can become a habit with particular classes; they (the class) may not realise how loud or disturbing they are. Any solution to the noise level problem will need to:

- address *the fundamental rules* (or classroom agreements) for communication, learning and fair treatment.
- *teach* the class what we mean by reasonable noise level.
- gain their *ownership* of any solution.

Peer support
Where the 'noise' situation concerns more than several students, the solution is best developed through peer-support approaches. Explore the various different solutions with colleagues who teach the same class. Simply yelling at the class every few minutes is counter-productive and will, in fact, only make matters worse.

The noise meter
We've used this at primary and middle school levels. You need to make a large cardboard disc with four colour quadrants, white, green,

amber and red, and an arrow that can spin (from the central axis). Explain that:

> 'This will be our noise meter. White is for quiet activities and up-front class discussion time (hands up without calling out). Green is for quiet and reasonable working noise when everyone can work without distraction. Amber is a warning — I won't say anything, I'll just put the arrow to amber and expect you to bring the noise back to the 'green-level' working noise. Red means you've gone too far. We all stop and we refocus.'

Noise monitors can be elected by the class, to keep an eye on the noise meter; this is especially effective when students work in groups.

A chart can also be used to record scores: 10 points if we can stay in green all the lesson, 5 points if we come back from amber to green zone without teacher direction. The teacher can then set a target number of points and the class can choose a free activity (a quiet free activity) as a reward when the target is reached.

Trade off

Another useful strategy is to use a trade off: we work quietly (reasonable working noise) for the next X minutes (30 minutes at secondary level) and the last five minutes we can have social chat time (with books away). At least we'll get a more productive 30 minutes of on-task time.

Other solutions

Another useful strategy (within collegiate support) is to run a classroom meeting (see p. 133), encouraging students to come up with solutions.

If it's more serious and long term we'll have to employ 'cracking the hard class' syndrome (see p. 143-9).

KEEPING THE CLASS BACK

Keeping the class back for misdemeanours (noise level, silly behaviour, time-wasting) is a common but unhelpful practice. Students rightly moan about it as unjust.

An exception to this would be where a session's immediate concern needs resolving *before* the class leaves. A piece of equipment clearly missing in textiles, a student's work ripped up, a teacher's car keys pinched....

When no one owns up and the class clams up, what are our options?

1. If you've got a good relationship with the class, say (five minutes before the bell) 'I'm going to stand outside the door and wait for three minutes and I want my keys (or the piece of equipment, or...) or my desk. No questions asked.'

   A variation of this approach is to give everyone a sheet of paper, get them to write the perpetrator's name (and comment if they wish) and collect them up. If the class is too unsettled, call in a senior member to go through a weeding-out process.

2. Send immediately for a senior staff member. Make it sound serious. The senior staff member (using a pre-arranged plan) walks in and says, 'There is a piece of equipment missing' (or 'Someone's work has been ripped up and I want to know who has done it so it can be fixed', or 'Someone has Ms Davies' keys...') 'Now, I don't want to keep any of you longer than necessary...' (make it sound as if you're on their side). 'I'll call each of you up in turn and ask you if you did it. If you say no I'll turn and ask the class if that is true. If you all agree I'll ask that person to go and wait with Ms Davies outside. Do you understand?' Of course, the senior staff member will pick on the 'safe' students first. Normally a pool of 'possibles' is left who are quite happy to 'rat on one another'.

3. An alternative is the longer-winded interview process of cross-checking stories.

SWEARING

Swearing, the frustration-engendered stuff, is more common in playgrounds and corridors but occurs sometimes in the classroom. Also 'common' is 'conversational' swearing, the easy slipping into sh.., f..., or a...hole. Now and then teachers will be faced with provocative swearing between students or even addressed at them.

- It is important to **distinguish** the frustration-type swearing, as when a student drops something and says sh..! and swearing as abuse.
- **Distinguish** between the social inappropriateness of swearing and how you can effectively deal with it at the classroom and out-of-classroom level (corridor, playground excursion).

- **Address** frustration and conversational swearing differently from swearing as a personal attack. Not all swearing is the same. Of course, teachers' values about swearing varies but swearing *per se* cannot hurt us or enrage us (as it does some teachers) unless we attribute some magic of hurt to the four-letter provocateurs!

A colleague of mine tells the story of a teacher who literally dragged a student by the arm into the principal's office demanding blood. 'What happened?' asked the principal. 'He called me a silly old cow just because I told him to clean up!' 'Did he shout it at you face to face?' 'No I was lucky to hear it!' The principal made the point that some swearing is not worth 'hearing' on the spot — it can be followed up later.

- **Plan ahead**, discuss with your colleagues, how to address the issue without soap-box preaching and moralising. ('I don't care what you say when you're at home, but in my class you will not swear, do you understand!!!') Over-dwelling on the incident is guaranteed to blow it out of proportion. If the swearing is directed at another student or you, deal with it as provocation by assertive direction.
- Some swearing can be **tactically ignored**. If you barely hear it as you move round the room (and especially in corridor or playground), it can be tactically ignored. If every piece of *sotto voce* swearing was addressed in the playground we'd be 'head cases' in a week. Loud swearing or provocative swearing needs a clear reminder that 'In our school we have a rule for positive language and we expect you to use it, thanks (smile)'. The firmness of the tone depends on the kind of swearing used.
- If it occurs in the 'up-front' stage, a *brief* reminder of the language rule is enough, then redirect the class back to the lesson or activity.
- If it occurs during 'on-task' time, remind the student of the rule or distract him or her aside to remind where possible that we all get uptight and frustrated, but there are other things we can say (wink).

Little Matthew is frustrated with his textile pattern in Year 3 art. He says (he's heard this at home) 'Holy shit!' and slams it down sulking (low frustration tolerance). The teacher doesn't give a lecture on swearing (what good would that do?) nor does he refer to the child's home background (public shaming). He briefly reminds Matthew of the class rule and redirects him to the work. 'Matthew, we've got a class rule. Good language, no swearing. I can see you're having trouble. Come on, let's have a look....' Later he'll have a chat with him about swearing and give alternatives.

Where swearing becomes frequent in the student's behaviour, contact agreements and parent conferences may help.

Defusing through humour

One of my colleagues overheard a student use the epithet 'smartarse'. Coming over he asked, 'What did you say? (a grin on his face). 'I, I...said smart*arms*.' 'Oh, that's good. I wouldn't want you to be an *arms*hole.' Repartee is not everyone's forte but it is a powerful way to defuse any interpersonal heat. Later remind the student of more appropriate social language.

I've had 'tough' attention-seekers bait me with 'This work's shit.' bending down I sniff it and wink, 'You could be right.'

'Cow' is muttered behind the teacher's back. She walks over. 'Michael,' (he looks up guiltily) 'Moo!' she says smiling, 'and I'll see you after class.'

'Bugger this...' says David as he seeks to master the coping saw. The teacher comes over and says, 'I didn't know you could do that with a saw.' Welcome laughs, tension defused, the teacher redirects the student on how to use the saw and has a *brief* chat about positive language, leaving with a wink and smile. It becomes no big deal.

Interpersonal swearing

If swearing is used interpersonally in the classroom, use an assertive (bit of emotion) statement, for example, 'Neil, that's a put down and put downs hurt' (emphasis on the name), or, 'Neil, we've got a rule for respect (or positive language) and I expect you to use it!'

If they argue, redirect: 'Yeah, but yer didn't hear what Katie said to me did you!?' 'Maybe I didn't, but we've got a class rule for respect....' Then defer apologies to an after-class situation when the heat has gone down.

The teacher hears David call Anna a 'slut':

T   David, [pause for effect and attention] that's a put down, and
       put downs hurt [or] David, we've got a class agreement for
       respect, I expect you to use it.
S   Gees, I was only joking.
T   Maybe you think it was a joke but we've got a rule for respect
       and I expect you to use it.

If he still protests, let him know we can follow it up after class. If it is a quiet put down or harassing behaviour (sly variety), direct the student aside and discipline him on a more 'private' basis. Tell him what you saw and/or heard and remind him of the rule. If it continues the consequences will be.... If he argues, redirect.

It is unhelpful to force apologies at the point of conflict. Defer apologies by calling both students back (when the heat has gone down) after class and go through the 4Ws (p. 92). If there is not time after class use a scheduled time to go over this issue — it demonstrates your serious concern about this form of behaviour. Do not hesitate to seek senior teacher support if you're not sure how best to follow the issue through.

Harassment deserves our justified anger. Students need to know this is not acceptable here — at all.

Swearing at teacher

If swearing is used at a teacher, either use a strong assertive 'I' statement or exit the student from the classroom. The school may have a policy statement on swearing at teachers. If so, use it but be sure to follow up with the student some time after the incident.

'Neil, you know I don't speak like that to you and I don't expect you to speak like that to me. I'm not into stand-up aggro, OK?' The teacher and student can then work on a plan with the student to gain agreement on apology (without rancour) and future behaviour. If the student says 'sorry' (often cursory), ask what will happen next time he is uptight when similar conditions occur.

HARASSMENT

Harassment whether sexual, racial, or bullying, is no light matter. People's self-esteem and morale is undermined even when the harassment is verbal or suggestive. Students and teachers have the right to *feel* safe at school (emotionally safe in terms of fundamental dignity). Mutual rights are the context within which the addressing of harassment occurs. In terms of a whole-school policy, it needs to be spelled out what harassment is and why it is totally unacceptable. The school, through class teachers, need to discuss the issue and deal decisively with it when it occurs. It is behaviour that cannot be ignored — it has to be addressed.

Having a clear, 'open' policy available to all members of the school community is an essential basis for effective discipline when harassment occurs. Students and staff need to know what it is, why it's wrong, and what the school's due process is for dealing with it. It is advisable to appoint a school-wide 'equal opportunity officer' to keep the policy process active within the school.

Harassment, generally, may be defined as any non-verbal, verbal or physical conduct which is uninvited, unreturned, often repeated, and also unprovoked. As Smith and Thomson (1991) note with respect to bullying (as harassment), the hurt 'can be both physical and/or psychological' (p. 1). It is unwise to treat harassment lightly or to trivialise it. ('These things happen you know — they're only joking!' 'Oh boys will be boys.').

Sexual harassment
Sexual harassment can range from leers, stares, signals, calling names, suggestive comments about one's person or sexual behaviour, offensive jokes to purposeful physical contact. It is at the 'subtle' level that it is most difficult to address. If it is the teacher on the receiving end, address it firmly, decisively.

An assertive response
One of my (female) colleagues taught Craig, who fancied himself as something of a stud, who leered and winked and (slyly) suggested (in class) that she might like to go out with him. He also (*sotto voce*) commented on her great body....

The first time it happened she called him aside, just outside the door, and said, 'I don't like it when you wink at me. I don't like it when you make comments about my body. I don't like it when you talk about me going out with you. I want it to stop, now!'

Her voice was firm, clear, decisive, unambiguous. Her eye contact unwavering.

He stumbled over his words as he said, 'I, I, I....was only mucking around.' (The sad part is that in his private, twisted logic that might be true.)

My colleague replied, 'Maybe you were but I want it to stop now do you hear?' He butted in again, she repeated, 'Do you hear?'

He did. Next day it was forgotten and she was able to re-establish a working relationship with him.

The longer we leave subtle sexual harassment the more difficult it becomes. Assertive approaches are very effective and ought to be part of any counselling programme for student and or teacher victims. If victims can assert strongly the offender may not try it again. Simply arguing or crying may only feed their pathetic ego. Many subtle forms of harassment (and put downs) are not seen by students in the same way as teachers. When I've addressed students who use words like slut head, poofter, slag, mole, dickhead, they protest that they're only joking. 'Anyway he's my mate...' While our values may be different from some 'street-values', I believe we need to point out (whole-class meetings are a good vehicle) that these sorts of behaviours affect rights of dignity, safety and respect.

Grievance procedures
More explicit forms — such as pinching, direct touching (falling towards someone, or on someone), repeated requests to 'go out', 'flashing', showing of sexually explicit material, invitation to sexual favours — cannot be tolerated. A due process for grievance needs to be set in place *at the earliest moment* if an assertive stance does not see an end to it.

- Confidential reporting.
- Documentation through the equal opportunity officer and head teacher; due 'right of reply' given (the victim ought to be allowed an advocate if they feel distressed or frightened).
- Consequences will be applied and counselling will be given.

This grievance procedure should be published policy and used whenever a person feels they have a case for harassment.

CLASSROOM MEETINGS

Essentially a classroom meeting is a problem-solving or discussion forum to enable the class to focus on an issue and as a class group to come up with recommendations, procedures, aims, strategies or appropriate consequences for behaviour. For example, if the teacher is receiving complaints about, or is noticing, behaviours such as students 'putting each other down', mess in class, irresponsible behaviour, noise level, a class meeting is an ideal forum for problem-solving:

- It shares responsibility for problem solving and management *with* the class groups.
- It can demonstrate that you believe the students can take ownership over problems and concerns.
- It demonstrates your concern; students are (all at the *same time*) made aware of a teacher's or other students' concern.

This model of problem-solving is well established in the literature and is common practice in a number of primary schools.

It is important to remember that this approach is a *skill*. If you have never used it before it will be advisable to discuss with a colleague how you will go about using it, perhaps even running a meeting together. Your students may not have been used to such an approach. There are skills for them to learn too:

- listening to others' points of view without criticising;
- turn taking, active listening;
- evaluation rather than judgement;
- making *shared* decision.

Seating

It is often more effective to have the seating arranged in a circle. Ask the students prior to the meeting for ideas on how best to move desks to the side and arrange the chairs in a circle. Practice is the best solution.

Set rules for class meetings

- 'One at a time' hands up, or use the green/white card at primary level (small card with green on one side white on the other, 'show the card to green if you want to make a point').
- Listen when others speak and remember 'we're here to address the problem not attack the person' (no put downs).
- Stay on the topic in hand.
- We decide together about solutions.

Consequences

If the class meeting is to decide classroom consequences for particular behaviours (swearing, being late, teasing, 'put downs', persistent calling out) be sure to emphasise that the solution (the consequence) should be reasonable (just), related (it should fit the behaviour in an if...then way) and should respect the person (Nelson 1987). These are 'tests' for class decisions about consequences.

Length of meeting

A meeting time of 15–20 minutes is normally enough to discuss an issue (if going well it can extend to 30 minutes). If not the issue can be deferred until another meeting. Many students have not experienced teachers treating ownership in a serious way like this. They are used to the teacher making all the decisions. It may need a few meetings to get this point across (there is important learning in the process itself).

When to call a meeting
Meetings can be conducted when a class needs to discuss a problem behaviour, a problem student (it may be advisable for the student to be out of the room at the time), a forthcoming unit of work, classroom chores (monitors), a concern raised by student/s. A number of primary schools have a weekly (20 minutes) meeting and take up issues on a bulletin board on display in the room. Meetings can also be run when important events or changes take place in a class. A new unit of work, a new way of working as a group (co-operative learning, teams, goal-based assessment); an excursion; a forthcoming camp (planning rules, consequences, activities).

Reorientation
Class meetings can also be used to reorient a class. Where a class has built up a 'hard-class' reputation, the teacher (with a support colleague) can conduct a meeting to focus on these three questions:

- What's going well, what's working well in this class?
- What's not working well and why?
- What can we do to change things? and how?

Teacher skills
For a classroom meeting to be successful, a teacher needs to restrain the more outspoken, draw out the more reticent and be able to clarify suggestions and enable the class to move towards a reasonable decision. This takes some skill — all the skills described in Chapter 3 are relevant to this kind of meeting. Like any new or different strategies, practice will help. It can also be instructive to sit in with a teacher who uses such meetings on a regular basis.

Conduct of meeting
During the meeting, list the suggestions, ideas, recommendations (or ask a student to do it, preferably on a visible board). Choice of solution should be democratic and the solution itself achievable.

'Difficult' students
If the meeting is to address a particular child (bully, extreme attention-seeker) it will be politic to have the child out of the room. Many

teachers have successfully helped difficult children by asking for help from the class — with dignity and translating the plan back to the difficult student/s.

Summary: Classroom meetings

1. Decide what the topic for discussion is *or*

   Decide if you want to use the group as a role-playing exercise or self-esteem activity *or*

   Whether you want sub-groups to discuss an issue with the teacher moving around to assist.
2. Decide what time. A vote may decide the time allocation.
3. Decide how you get the chairs/desks moved into a circle.
4. Establish the rules quickly and reinforce them.
5. Define the topic clearly.
6. Keep the group meeting on task; draw the threads/ideas together; encourage a positive decision that reflects the rights/rules/responsibility focus of the classroom.

The essence of a classroom meeting is to open up and guide discussion towards responsible choices within the established rights and rules.

PLAYGROUND MANAGEMENT

I was doing my playground duty (not the most exciting of teacher duties). I noticed (how could I miss him?) a student riding a bike around the asphalt area in the vicinity of small children. He saw me coming and got off. I hadn't asked him to get off; he started to move towards me. 'Hello. What's your name?' He stopped and, giving me a sullen look, said 'Damien'. Even before I began to address the rule-breaking behaviour his voice carried residual hostility (he would have been 12 or 13 years of age.)

T   Damien, what's the rule for riding bikes in the playground? [My tone was pleasant, my eye contact was direct even if his skewed away.]

S   I dunno. [His answer, his pouting face and tone were quite out of proportion to what I was addressing.]

T   I do — the rule is we walk our bikes or store them by the shed. Riding isn't allowed on this play area. [A low level of assertion, even pleasantness in my voice. The 'secondary behaviour' continued.]

S   Gees! I'm not the only one riding me bike? [A whining, rising inflection, as he pointed to a student way off in the distance near the school fence also riding his bike.]

T   I see him. But what are you supposed to be doing with your bike on school property? [I kept the focus on the primary issue.]

S   The other day Mr _____ said it was all right.

T   Maybe he did... but what's the rule?

S   Walk my bike! [In a 'sing song' voice.]

T   OK, walk it thanks. [At this I walked away — expecting his compliance. He did]

At the end of 1991 I joined a barbecue with one of the schools where I do demonstration teaching. I was, again, on playground duty. As I walked along the path I heard a boy working up a gurgling, heavy, spit. I turned in time to direct him to 'lob' it into the bushes. He grinned. In that school if we see a student 'lob' it on the path, teachers direct the student to get some paper towelling from the toilets and wipe it up (a brief explanation that it's a health issue). If they argue, we redirect. If they still argue we ask for their name and follow it through with the year-level coordinator out-of-class at another time, as is necessary, and clean up that area then. Many though will wipe it up on the spot (it's a bad habit).

As I emerged onto the asphalt play area I saw a student throwing a large paper plate (smeared with sauce) around like a Frisbee. A small group of boys (Year 8s or 9s) were watching, laughing. I walked over towards the boys tactically ignoring the 'plate-tosser'. I asked them the name of the boy tossing the plate several metres from us. 'Him? That's Max.'

T   [I called him over.] Max, see you for a moment? [He eyeballed me with surprise that I knew his name. I turned to the other boys (communicating the expectation that I believed he would come over) and started to chat about the Christmas holidays. He didn't come, he diverted his energy to a stick on the ground which he picked up proceeding to hit the plate.]

T   [I called again.] Max, see you for a moment? [Again I returned (abstractedly) to the conversation with the smaller group. He sidled over.]

S   Yeah. What d'you want. [His voice was redolent of the cheeky challenge, his arms folded, his legs askew.]

T   I want you to pick the plate up please [I pointed] and drop it in the bin.

S   S'not my plate! [Secondary behaviour]
T   Maybe it isn't, but I'd like you to drop it in the bin — Ta. [At
        this I turned aside to continue my 'other' conversation as if he'd
        in fact do it. He walked over to the plate and hit it with his stick,
        he poked it, jabbed it and finally dropped it, grumbling, into the
        waste bin. All through the episode I was tactically ignoring him
        as I chatted with the others. As the plate hit the bin, I turned
        and simply said] Ta, Max.

Keeping the focus on the primary issues is not easy unless you are
conscious of your language, the tone and expectation and being aware
of how to proceed from a least to most intrusive stance.

   In both of these instances, had the students refused to 'own' their
behaviour (within the fair rules) we could apply the choice consequence
(see p. 90) deferring the follow up to a time when the audience isn't
around.

Rewards for good behaviour

One approach to positive consequences in the playground (at primary
level) is the handing out of red sashes. On playground duty teachers
carry a small bucket with red sashes, and award them — discriminately
— to students they see picking up litter (without being asked), acting
co-operatively in their play, helping a student (specially an older to
younger student) who is in difficultly or who has fallen over.... When I
first saw this (as a consultant to the school) I thought the students
would see it as a bit of a 'game'. Not so. It has significantly increased
positive social behaviours. Of course, it relies on a teacher's
discriminating eye. The children then proudly wear their 'earned'
sash back to their class; their teacher notes it on a chart and five
notings earns a certificate of merit. The students love it. Even difficult
students can earn a ribbon.

   On one of my playground duties there, I observed two small boys pick
up a couple of ribbons that had been dropped accidentally by my
colleague. From, a distance I saw them slip them over their heads.
Walking up behind them I said, 'Hi boys, what did you get your ribbons
for? One of them looked sheepish, the other giggled. I repeated the
question, 'Nice ribbons, what did you get them for?' Little Peter grinned,
'Mr Williams, he dropped them and we put 'em on.' 'Well,' I said,
'That's honesty. It isn't easy being honest. I appreciate that. Well —
you've earned them.' The smiles returned. They went back and told their
teacher they had earned their ribbons for being honest!

DUTY OF CARE OUTSIDE THE CLASSROOM

The moment we leave our classroom, as we walk down corridors, across the playground, whether we are 'on duty' or not, we have a duty of care. Some teachers walk down corridors and across the playground, or stand around on bus duty, or wet day duty, and take the 'two monkeys position' (hear no evil, see no evil).

Running in corridors, eating in 'no-eating' areas, pushing against lockers, spitting, out of bounds play, 'silly' play, toilet hassling (intimidation and crowding), litter (residual and intentionally dropped), smoking, teasing, tale-telling, fighting.... At what point should we address these? If so, how? What if the student challenges us? Students feel that once they are out of the confines of the classroom they are in 'their territory', 'free' in a sense from the constraints of the classroom. Teachers are much more likely to be challenged in this arena than any other. Witness the normal litter scene:

A teacher in the playground sees several students sitting on a seat with residual litter around their feet — whose is it?

T   Right, come on, pick this up [He says, eye-balling one of the triumvirate].

Ss   S'not ours!

T   I don't care whose it is, come on, pick it up.

Ss   Why should we? [In this sense the students are right. If it's not theirs, why should they pick it up *just because* a teacher says so? Conversely, it could be a ruse.]

I've seen teachers get into a lather when students challenge them on issues like litter, no-ball areas, running in corridors, swearing, even when (rarely) students refuse to give their name, or give a false name.

I asked a student recently (he was flicking small stones around) for his name. I do this to 'break the ice' when addressing 'low-level' disruptions. 'Guess!' he answered with a cheeky grin. I winked, 'I could guess all day — I won't — just want to remind you of our safety rules, OK?' 'I'm just mucking around!' he said. 'I'm sure you are (redirection) but in this group (there were a couple of other boys and a few girls) it could get into someone's eyes easily, OK?' There was the normal giggling as I moved away with 'see you later'. With regard to students' names, 'forcing' them out of them is pointless in a public area. Follow up later through the year-level co-ordinator. Have an eye for faces when they challenge your *reasonable* teacher direction, reminder or question. Then follow up later. It's the certainty of follow up that's important, the message will finally get through.

Walking up to several students (whom I had taught earlier that day), 'Bit of litter?' I said, scanning the group. 'It's Michael and Sean, isn't it?' Looking at the litter they gave the standard reply, 'Yeah, but we didn't drop it.' 'No doubt, but I'd like you to help me do the playground a favour (wink and smile) OK? I'll pick it up with you. We can clean it all up in less that a minute.' They responded to this jockeying (languorously). I rarely have any problem using this approach even at secondary level. Confrontation is unnecessary.

Several students are running to the exit door to go back in after the play bell has rung. Here is a time to raise the 'Oi!', a sharp, brief, attention-getter. As the several running students turn around, call them over. 'OK fellows (you guessed it, boys again!), let's *walk* in, thanks.' A brief rule reminder; it's worth it. They might think twice next time. Simple reminders are useful for corridor running and loud swearing. 'Oi!' or 'Excuse me' at a louder pitch raises attention, then drop the voice, 'Walking in the corridor thank you.' I'll often draw students aside in corridors when there is loud swearing and just remind them of the rule. 'We've got a school rule for positive language, let's use it thanks.' If they prevaricate, redirect. If you know their name, use it, if not ask a student nearby.

I saw a student holding another boy in a neck lock during a playground game. I asked some student nearby who the student with the striped top was. 'Oh him, that's Peter.' I called Peter over, 'Peter, see you for a moment?' Surprised I knew his name, he walked over to where I was abstractedly chatting with other students. 'Yeah, what do you want?' 'Peter, what game are you playing?' 'Rugby,' he replied a little sulkily. 'Yes, I noticed, but that heavy wrestling can get out of hand, football is safer.' 'I was only mucking around.' 'I'm sure you were but football is safer and it doesn't need headlocks (wink). Enjoy your game.' He went away muttering. Next time on playground duty I remembered his name and said 'Hi.' This brief re-establishing says, 'no hard feelings'.

Having a plan

It is important for teachers to have a '*duty of care plan*' for use in corridors, on bus duty, lunch duty, excursions, school camps, playground duty and in assemblies. The features of any plan are:

- Conscious awareness of the 'public' area in which we have to discipline (on a bus, in a corridor, in a playground with the coterie watching); and emphasising to all staff the importance of active supervision, especially at primary level.

- Have a least to most intrusive approach for reminding and corrective discipline, have some known, discussed rules.
- Have some prepared language repertoire for the common situations.
- Know how you'll get support for difficult situations (students on the roof, students who run away, fights that get out of hand).

School survey and review

One way to achieve a *school-wide consistency* is to survey staff and students on common concerns for playground misbehaviour, where the 'hot' spots in the playground (and inside school buildings) are and then formulate an out-of-classroom management plan. There ought to be an expectation that teachers (whether 'on duty' or not) will deal with misbehaviour in as consistent a manner as possible.

- Survey staff to find out what are the *most* frequent (but low-serious) behaviours they have to face in their duty of care role. Are there any particular areas they notice that are more troublesome? Why? Any age group causing more problems? Any names crop up? (The sub-terrorists, bullies or victims?) Also survey on low frequency but high-serious behaviours.
- Survey students through class teacher (primary) or group tutor (secondary) playground concerns. What's working well and why? What concerns do they have and why? What can we do to improve things? (This includes equipment, better litter bins, seating, play areas and so on.)
- A steering committee collates this to begin a policy review. Are the rules clear? Are they positively (behaviourally) stated? Do they need modifying? Do the students know them? How? One school I've been working with has a whole wall, just inside the foyer, with illustrations by students on key rules for playground and corridor. The fundamental rights that need protecting in the playground are safety and treatment. Can I feel safe? Can I be treated fairly and with respect? (Racism, sexist behaviour, put downs, intimidation and any form of bullying are totally unacceptable).

Dealing with all forms of bullying has to be a whole-school issue addressing administration procedures, supervision and discipline procedures, use of consequences (even separate supervised play times as an extreme consequence), and educational measures (personal, social, moral education programmes) to set up an ethos and set of social expectations inimical to bullying (see the excellent text by Smith and Thompson 1991).

Strategies

Having listed most frequent (and low serious) to least frequent (and high serious) concerns, staff in small groups can suggest strategies for dealing with teasing, litter, tale-telling (do we shoo them off or give them a simple plan?), swearing, out of bounds... right through to fighting.

These strategies should be simple, least to most intrusive and positive (where appropriate), with clear options noted by staff as preferred practice — good practice as defined by the principles noted earlier. They should include ways to deal with conflict and argumentative students (especially those who refuse to follow reasonable teacher directions).

A plan for dealing with fighting is essential, even the distinguishing of silly male play-fighting (that can get out of hand) through to the bloody-nose jobs. Some inner-city schools I work with have playground duty in pairs plus a red card (carried by teachers) to send to the office in an emergency. Not all teachers are confident to physically separate heavy fighters who refuse a direct command. It is important to have a back-up support process for crisis situations.

It is also important for staff to be aware that positive encouragement and reinforcement is appropriate in the playground.

Consequences

Schools need to develop a plan for appropriate consequences for each of the duty-of-care situations. For example, is a time-out bench appropriate at primary school level? Or sending a student in from play? What happens if a student runs away and refuses to be directed inside? Will we instruct rostered litter duty for all students? Have we surveyed the students and the student council to get the advice? Using the principle of least to most intrusive, what consequences ought to follow on from a playground incident? Who is responsible for the follow up? It is advisable for the duty of care teacher to follow through after the 'event' to indicate to students that they can't merely play one teacher off against another. This needs clear collegial back-up.

Publishing the plan
The duty of care plan (especially playground, corridor, wet day and lunch supervision) needs to be published and all staff will need regular in-service training each year. Younger students will need to be involved in an intensive programme outlining safety in the playground, ways of playing games, how to use equipment, no-ball areas. Students new to the school will need to know these procedures and routines too.

If you're in a school with no published or clear policy, check with your head of department as to what the process is.

Environment
It is important for the school administration to work on the corridor and playground environment. Some schools are Dickensian when it comes to aesthetics. Work on carpeting corridors (it reduces noise), students' work illustrating corridor walls on fixed boards with perspex covers (some secondary corridors are like the Lubianka!), seating in playgrounds in circular arrangements rather than cheap wooden benches fixed along a wall, trees, potted shrubs, attractive school entrances with comfortable seats for parents/visitors, a coffee table with school magazines, photo albums, etc., decent (and ample) rubbish bins (with windproof lids), play equipment that is safe, marked areas for games, etc. It costs, but it's worth it.

CRACKING THE HARD CASES

Most schools have a small percentage of very difficult to manage students. Their recidivism is wearing to students and staff alike. They tend to have:

- a social-emotional deficit;
- a significant lack of social skill;
- a *persistence* in their disruptive behaviour, a severity in the degree of hostility or acting out behaviours (often males).

When the frequency, intensity and duration of a student's behaviour has resisted normal and reasonable discipline, counselling and support measures, a school will need to consider formal enquiry and suspension procedures. A school will need to have assessed such students on a team approach. *Support* is the key, especially staff support. (Some principals forget how difficult these students can be in a class-audience setting).

A whole-school approach

It is essential that, when such a student is identified, the teachers who have duty of care receive adequate support. The key to effective management is peer support: a common plan, a consistent plan.

At primary level all specialist teachers will work with the class teacher and deputy principal to develop an agreed approach which will include:

1. A class plan for discipline that has a well-established time-out procedure (see pp. 95-100).
2. Partial time-release from that student for the class teacher (we've often rotated such students between several teachers to ease the pain).
3. Partial enrolment if appropriate.
4. Parent conferencing and counselling (working with the parents where possible on a joint plan and support).
5. Use of very simple contracts that re-emphasise rights and responsibilities (especially safety of other children).
6. A curriculum that caters for the wide ability range. We can consider:
   - simple, progressive, work contracts;
   - a range of 'learning centres' around the room (a small table with a poster illustrating the 'learning centre task'); the learning centre tasks can be language activities, puzzles, maths activities, which are challenging and interesting and can be pursued individually or in pairs;
   - co-operative learning strategies where students do some of their learning activities in mixed-ability groups (see Dalton 1985);
   - cross-age tutoring — having (an) older child/ren from upper years working with younger children;
   - class mentors, where students sit with classmates and give individual assistance;
   - back-up support for children with significant problems with literacy and numeracy; behaviour and learning problems are often correlated; some one-to-one withdrawal is necessary to strengthen these children's skills in literacy and numeracy and to *build confidence and self-esteem.*
7. A plan for dealing with anti-social playground behaviour on a team basis.

8. Professional development in the skills necessary for dealing with such students.

Balancing these students' rights to an education needs to be balanced with other students', and teachers', rights. Those outside the profession have little idea how taxing such students are on the emotional health of a teacher, and class.

At the secondary level a year-level co-ordinator will facilitate a year-level plan (see pp. 105-6).

Some schools appoint a reference group to facilitate any due process so that subject teachers have a 'common' plan and feel supported if they need to use time out (see pp. 95-100).

CRACKING THE HARD CLASS

A 'reputation' class whose *esprit de corps* seems designed to cause maximum strain and pain can occur at any year level. Again a whole-school, whole-year, approach may be necessary. If a skewed grouping of students is identified by several teachers (rather than one) a team approach will enable staff to:

- Have an *appropriate forum* to share their frustration 'Oh you too...!').
- *Identify common concerns.* Any ringleaders? Any sub-terrorist groups? Is their behaviour consistently problematic across all subject areas? What specific behaviours do teachers complain of?
- Identify *what strategies they've tried* in managing the class and its individuals. Any success, any obvious (repetitive) failures? (Why keep doing the same thing if it's failing?) This data will help each teacher, and the team, to develop a common action plan.

There is a natural frustration at such meetings. It will be important to avoid blaming — the meeting is geared to support and problem-solving. It will be important for the facilitator to plan ahead for dealing with the very angry, the very upset, the cynic. Even experienced teachers have problems with 'reputation classes'. Teachers will need to acknowledge:

1. There is a problem with 8D or 7E!
2. Help for teachers is needed.
3. *That* help is best developed through mutual support.

Bringing in a senior teacher to read the Riot Act may temporarily assuage things but it does little for the teacher's self-esteem. It is unlikely that a class will change on the strength of a ten-minute lecture! It is important, too, at the secondary level not to skew these classes to first-year teachers or those new to the school. If there is a clear 'reputation' class, the more experienced teacher should be given the weightier time-table loadings.

Look for solutions
- Can we split off any of the clear ringleaders or even split the group?
- Can any of the learning curriculum strategies be realistically modified?
- Run a classroom meeting, with the support of a colleague (see pp. 133-4, 146-7).

Classroom meeting
Arrange the seating in a half circle. Warn the class beforehand of the specific issues of concern you'll be discussing at the next class session (noise levels, specific put downs, calling out during instruction time, seat-wandering, and so on). At the meeting use an 'open' or 'closed' format.

'Closed' format
Outline to the class the *specific* areas of concern. These can be listed on a sheet, which is given out, as well as on the board. Indicate that this serious state cannot go on. Re-establish the class rules *and* consequences (listed), and invite comment. Explain how time out and parent referral may be used (see pp. 95-100).

With this approach, it is better if the meeting is handled by the year-level co-ordinator and each subject teacher is given feedback on how the meeting went.

'Open' format
This type of meeting can operate with *each* subject teacher if necessary. The class are asked to respond to the three Ws:

- What's working well in this class and why (be specific)?
- What's not working well and why (be specific)?
- What do we need to do to change things for the better?

This can be carried out as an individual pen and paper exercise by students, or in small groups, or as whole class 'brain-storming'.

Mini-meets
This is another option, where the class teacher withdraws three students at a time while a colleague takes the class.

Stop/start contracting
Withdraw the power-brokers and ringleaders and develop individual behaviour contracts with them indicating the behaviours they need to stop and start. These contracts will need to be discussed and 'owned', and should be simple and achievable (two or three specific behaviour areas). The student should be given regular feedback by the co-ordinator and subject teachers. The questions asked will be, 'Are these behaviours helping you in class or causing you problems? What do you (specifically) need to do to be more successful in class, and how can I help?'

Observation and feedback
In less severe cases, teachers can work on mutual peer observation and feedback in each others' classes with this problem group. The observations need to be specific and non-judgemental.

Group reinforcement
The class can be split into mixed-ability groups (by secret ballot) and points allocated for working by class rules and co-operative on-task behaviours. The process can last over several weeks and then be phased out. Each group puts 'pressure' on its members to co-operate in order to earn team points under their leader. Most points are skewed to co-operative behaviours (see Rogers 1991, Barrish *et al.* 1969; Brown *et al.* 1974).

- *Emphasise novelty* through rewards. 'You can all earn points, in your group, to trade in for free-time activities and prizes' (novelty pens, stickers, comics, even 'teeth-rotters'!) Make it sound exciting!

- *Plan ahead* well to have charts for the allocation of points, the rules chart, expectations for co-operative behaviour. The class need to know what they'll earn points for as individuals *within* and *for* their teams. Teams, too, can earn points for being on task, co-operative, sticking to healthy working noise.

- *Select leaders* using a secret ballot. Small slips of paper are given out after the explanation of the 'new way we're going to work as a class'. 'Write down two names of a person you'd like to choose as a group leader.' Collect the slips up and choose four or five leaders from the most recurring names. While the class is doing some busy work write them up on the large chart (four or five columns).

- *Call up the leaders to choose their teams.* The chosen leaders will privately choose their team members (one at a time to give 'mixed ability') from a class list. These will go up in the chart.

- Send the leaders back to their seats for their first task — *forming themselves quietly into the four or five groups* as in the chart. Allocate areas of the room for the groups. Points will be put up on the chart for those working/moving the most quietly, and for the way they come in and go out of class. A point for an individual is allocated to the team, thus gaining group approval.

- Once the teams are spatially distinct (tables in groups, etc.), and settled, *thank them*. Show the teams they've already earned points for....

- Give them their normal (or alternate) class work to be done in a group context. In art/science/textile/technology classes, monitors get and distribute equipment, etc.

- *The teacher's role* is to encourage and reinforce on-task behaviours. Balance verbal encouragement with the points-on-the-chart allocation. Students need to get used to verbal reinforcement (pp. 42-4). It is also important not to take off points earned! All discipline is conducted within a planned approach including careful, supportive, use of time out (pp. 95f).

- *'Prizes' or 'rewards'* can be given on a sliding scale: 10 points for a team equals a teeth-rotter each, 20 points a free activity, 30 points a pen each, 50 equals afternoon tea! A list of rewards and prizes can go up next to the points chart. Any individual refusing to be part of the game (it happens rarely) can work alone and is welcome to join a group if they change their mind (pointless forcing them).

Lower primary groupings can also include group reinforcement ideas with group badges, group names, stickers, colourful cartoon charts, and so on. I've used group reinforcement with some very 'tough' groups up to Year 9. It relies on novelty, reorganising groupings, a balance of primary (the points allocated) and secondary reinforcement (what they 'trade' the points for), good humour and solid planning by the teacher — collegiate support to 'kick-start' the programme can help. I often end a six-to-eight week programme with a special class activity to celebrate our success (barbecue or morning or afternoon tea).

Summary
Any action plan for 'cracking a hard class' needs to involve significant peer support, to assess an action plan and give moral and organisational back-up. The goal is the same as with any discipline: to enhance behaviour ownership, accountability, respect for rights by the students and improvement in the learning climate.

8

A School-Wide Policy
Approach to Discipline and Student
Behaviour Management

A policy is, fundamentally, a statement of the school's beliefs and practices regarding behaviour management. It is important to know what your school's policy is on discipline:

- Is it written down? How old is it?
- Is it clear what *your* role in discipline is? What supports are available to you?

It is also important to have a *written* policy based on collaborative practices (survey staff, students, even parents!). A regular review of policy and yearly in-servicing of all staff is also important to enable a more consistent practice.

A DISCIPLINE FRAMEWORK

The *purpose* of any policy is to set a framework that corresponds to what a school will seek to practise. In the first instances the school community needs to make clear *what* discipline means. Is it just control by teachers? If so, what is legitimate control? (Pain, fear, even humiliation in the form of dunces' caps, etc. was *once* acceptable.) What do we seek to do when we discipline?

Within the definition of discipline used in this book, a school discipline policy provides a framework which:

- Establishes a stable social and learning environment.
- Encourages students to be responsible for their own behaviour, to develop self-discipline and enhance self-worth, and
- To respect the rights (and feelings) of others (fellow students and teachers).

- Sets out the school's expectations for rights-enhancing behaviour.
- Establishes a set of preferred practices, and due processes, for staff in addressing unacceptable student behaviour and student behaviour management generally.

Although **disruptive behaviour** can mean different things to different teachers (depending on frustration, tolerance, perception and skills), it can be defined as **behaviour that significantly affects fundamental rights to feel safe, to be treated with respect and to learn**. This encompasses behaviour that interferes with the rights and welfare of others, is offensive or inconsiderate, dangerous to person or property.

Preferred practices for student behaviour management and discipline need to be built on a sound philosophy of discipline and management rather than mere utility.

There are several areas a school discipline policy needs to address (see Fig. 5):

- The fundamental aims of discipline.
- The preferred practices or guiding principles by which we discipline (see. p. 153).
- A description of the relative roles of class teacher, middle and senior management — and even parents — in the application of discipline.
- Guidelines for classroom discipline (a discipline plan) to enhance consistency of practice (see Chapter 3).
- Guidelines for 'duty of care' outside the classroom (corridor supervision, lunch supervision, playground behaviour supervision, excursions, bus duty, wet-day duty).
- A school-wide time-out policy (see p. 95).
- A school-wide approach to the use of punishment with a preference towards consequences that are related and reasonable and maintained with due dignity (see p. 119).
- Use of behaviour contracts to enhance student self-control (see pp. 101-6).
- Use of counselling and welfare procedures to enhance discipline procedures.
- Guidelines for parent contact, referral and conferencing regarding student behaviour.
- A due process for extreme cases of disruptive behaviour – leading to sanctions such as suspension.
- Some policies usefully include a section on teacher welfare and

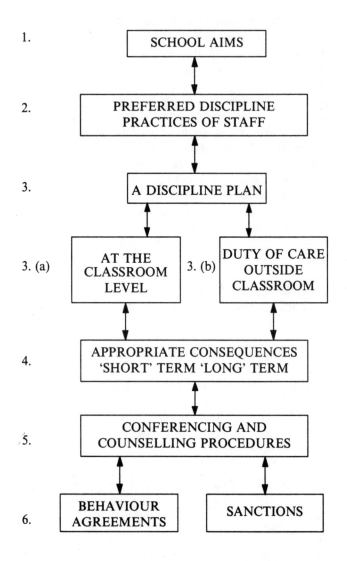

1. SCHOOL AIMS

2. PREFERRED DISCIPLINE PRACTICES OF STAFF

3. A DISCIPLINE PLAN

3. (a) AT THE CLASSROOM LEVEL

3. (b) DUTY OF CARE OUTSIDE CLASSROOM

4. APPROPRIATE CONSEQUENCES 'SHORT' TERM 'LONG' TERM

5. CONFERENCING AND COUNSELLING PROCEDURES

6. BEHAVIOUR AGREEMENTS

SANCTIONS

Fig. 5. Developing a school-wide framework
for positive discipline and student management

the school's approach to peer support (for staff).

Preferred practices

Preferred practices have been referred to in various ways in this text. They are summarised here as guiding principles for discipline school-wide:

- Discipline within *known* rights, responsibilities and fair rules at school-wide and classroom level. The features of school rules ought to reflect student input and discussion with students each year. The rules should be published in a positive style where possible and be related to rights and consequences.
- A management-discipline style based on assertion/consultation rather than confrontation. A balance between positive correction and encouragement ought to be the norm. Sarcasm, public (or private) embarrassment, shaming and ridicule, undue or persistent criticism is not appropriate or necessary.
- Avoid pushing students into pointless arguments. This is especially acute in a public forum (see pp. 25-9). In professional development of staff emphasis on assertion (as a skill) can enhance a more positive management style. A key feature of effective discipline and management is that of least to most intrusive (see p. 72) within a discipline plan.
- A school also needs to endorse the value of positive consequences for all students. Staff can discuss and set out how students can be encouraged in social and academic behaviour through verbal encouragement and the more formally recognised means.
- Separate the behaviour of the student from the student as a person. A standard conflict-resolution procedure is to attack the problem rather than the person.
- Teachers need to address student behaviour from the point of view of 'choice'. While the emotional pathology of some students is quite traumatic their behaviour is still their 'choice' — predisposed no doubt from emotionally strained home environments. Students can learn to make better choices and take responsibility for their own behaviour, and should be encouraged (and supported) to 'own' the outcomes of their behaviour and seek to fix it with teacher support and encouragement. To do this they will need to know what their rights and responsibilities are. The treatment *variable* is the key issue; once we start saying that students with problems *can't help* their behaviour we treat the student as a victim rather than an active agent who can be responsible with guidance (discipline) and support.

- A clear consensus on the nature and use of related consequences rather than mere punishment as the only tool for addressing disruptive behaviour. This will also need to encompass the use of appropriate cool-off time and time out in conflict situations (see p. 96).
- It is important for teachers to invite, model and expect respect rather than merely demand it.

Wider issues

The wider whole-school issues that a discipline welfare policy needs to address are:

- Social skills development (especially for children whose home life is one of socio-emotional deprivation).
- Pastoral care programmes built into the life of the school rather than merely tacked on.
- Cross-age tutoring.
- Student councils.
- The practice of classroom meetings to give students a decision-making forum.
- Student input into policy issues.
- The professional development of staff in the school policy especially new staff at the beginning of each year.

Children spend a third of their day at school. Giving them a sense of participation in *this* community can aid in the sense of 'ownership' they have in this place as a social as well as an academic institution.

A SUPPORTIVE CULTURE

Above all a school needs to encourage a supportive culture for staff. Peer support is essential in problem-solving and moral/emotional back-up when the going gets tough. A school can set out how peer support is utilised at the school, support that leads to:

- the assurance that one can be listened to with some understanding and empathy;
- staff welfare;
- supportive problem-sharing and solving;
- professional development in the areas noted in this text.

There will, of course, be many informal avenues for such support but school management can enhance the opportunity for peers to give support to one another. Peer support can:

- Create a climate where staff feel emotionally supported.
- Create a climate where staff feel they can raise, discuss and explore solutions collaboratively rather than become social isolates.
- Reduce organisational and work-related stress.
- Increase skill repertoire where staff develop skills through support rather than 'on their own'.

Staff will need to know that it is acceptable to seek support and to know *how* they can go about it. Senior staff will need to be sensitive in how they can offer colleagues emotional and practical support concerning discipline and management. Schools can enhance support by endorsing and enhancing a 'supportive culture':

- Structural support such as clear policies, on-going professional development, opportunities for raising issues in smaller forums at staff and faculty meetings.
- The opportunity for peer-support groupings on an ad hoc basis.
- Supportive feedback to staff concerning achievement as well as the opportunity for non-judgemental professional feedback.

Of course, support can be offered and invited, but it can't be forced.

It is especially important to give support to new teachers and supply teachers. Each school has its own 'culture' — cracking that culture isn't easy. A buddy system and a support group (if there are several new teachers) can ease them through the early days. Supply teachers need a summary of the discipline policy. Who is their referral person? What do they do for the 'reputation' class? They also need a clear map of the school with their room numbers marked, and basic information on break times, photocopier and phone usage, whether they're on playground duty, and any special procedures unique to student supervision. A sheet with the answers to their basic questions can be given them on arrival. It can also be helpful to introduce them to their class/es to enhance their status as a 'legit' teacher!

Developing a supportive culture is essential in a school. Social support has been identified as a key factor that enables teachers to cope with and manage stress. Researchers have consistently noted that individuals are in better shape mentally, and psychologically, when they have (and can utilise) peer support (Kryiacou 1981, 1987, Russell, Altmaier and Van Velzen 1987; Rogers 1991, 1992b).

As Oliver Sacks (1990, p. 268) has said, 'We cannot really separate individual endeavours from social endeavours.'

> Teachers have tended to stay out of each other's classrooms and not to talk about their own discipline problems. Too often teachers do not seek help because it feels like an admission of incompetence, and they do not offer it because it feels like accusing a colleague of incompetence. As a result the tradition of classroom isolation persists in many schools.
>
> The beliefs that either group management skills should not be necessary or that they cannot be learned seem to be traditional in parts of the profession. Our evidence suggests that these beliefs contribute significantly towards teacher stress. This is further increased by the more widespread tradition of classroom isolation. We see these beliefs or traditions as barriers to good teaching. They should be removed as quickly as possible.
>
> *The Elton Report (1989) p.69*

First-year teachers and peer support

Coming to a school as a first-year teacher is a culture shock. Already there is some natural apprehension of having one's 'own' classes, of fitting in with other teachers, of cracking the culture, of teaching as a career and the unique culture (ethos) of *this* school. Schools vary enormously in how supportive their culture is. Having worked with many first-year teachers I have seen for myself that they also lack fundamental management skills (Wheldall 1992) and need support in this area (Rogers 1992b):

- How to set up their first classes with simple, fair, workable rules and expectations.
- Setting up distribution and retrieval of class work.
- Beginning lessons and gaining (and maintaining) whole-group attention with a minimum of fuss.
- How to best organise room-seating; use of group work (how to do it).
- How to use positive corrective discipline on a least to most intrusive basis (see chapter 3).
- How to follow up students with consequences during and after class.
- When to refer difficult students.

It's easy to feel overwhelmed when new to the profession. Peer (collegiate) support can ease beginner teachers into their professional life. Even the basics such as internal communication procedures, who to ask for and when; use of photocopier (and how?); meeting times (faculty, staff, special needs, etc.); the timetable (how do you read it?!).

When you've been in a school a while the culture is almost 'second nature'. We forget the unease, the uncertainty, we felt at first. If newcomers are processed with 'Oh, the toilets are down there, here's the staff handbook and you've got double maths with 8D on Thursday afternoon...', little wonder there will be unnecessary stress. People feel less stressed when they have adequate information, or at least clear means for communication, and support. They feel better and more 'in control'. It is morally right and practically sensible to give structural support to first-year teachers and those new to the school.

- Arrange a peer-support group if there are a few new or first-year teachers. The aim of the group is to go over the issues of normal concern, giving them time to ask the basic (even 'dumb') questions. This group can meet (at least the first years) weekly for the first 6–8 weeks, then space it out as needs dictate. It is important to give early discussion and professional development time to the school's discipline and management policy, especially to allay the initial discipline concerns noted earlier. Prior to their first classes it can be supportive to give guidance on how to set up a discipline plan (Chapter 3). Having a second-year teacher sit in on the first meeting to share their experiences and impressions adds credibility to the support. Later meetings can concentrate on the teachers' direct concerns.
- If there is only one first-year teacher at the school he or she can either be part of a general peer-support group for all teachers new to the school or be encouraged to join in a regional support group (within that school cluster) with other first years. I have run many such groups and teachers rate the experience of meeting, discussing, sharing concerns, exploring solutions and gaining feedback as among the most significant professional assistance of their initial year (Rogers 1991a, 1992b).

Peer observation and feedback
One of the ways to improve one's skills is to form a group of like-minded individuals to discuss common classroom disruptions and solutions. Using the skills framework (see Chapter 3) we can discuss

how they might enhance classroom management.

We can invite a trusted colleague into some of the lessons to give us *targeted* feedback about our management and discipline. Feedback not judgement: it is what they see, hear and feel about our characteristic style. We plan what we'll observe, how we'll introduce our colleague to the class (low key) and how they will work with us through the lesson. We can then share our observations over a cuppa later.

Another way we can reflect on our practice is to use a good cassette recorder then play it back later (if our self-esteem can hack it!).

We can also use a reflective journal to record our impressions of what happened (specifically) and how effective we believed our discipline was. In the peer support group we can then share how our skill development is going. Developing skills through supportive feedback is one way to clarify the effectiveness of any change in our practice.

> We were given evidence that teachers often learn more about classroom skills by talking to each other than by listening to visiting 'experts'. A peer support group provides regular opportunities for sharing experiences and skills. Second, it helps to break down the tradition of isolation by opening the classroom door. Peer support groups can develop the kind of trust and confidence which leads to mutual observation and consultancy, which involves watching and commenting on each other's teaching. This is probably the most effective method of classroom skills training available. Third, it helps to reduce occupational stress. Knowing that even the most experienced teachers can have classroom management problems and that it is acceptable to admit to them is a good way of reducing stress. The feeling that it is possible to do something about those problems is even more reassuring.

> Teachers need, and in good schools receive, support from senior managers (head and deputies) and in secondary schools middle managers (heads of year or department), as well as peer support. The tradition of classroom isolation makes this difficult in two ways. Good teachers may get little or no recognition from senior staff for their achievements. This is demotivating. Professional etiquette may also leave teachers who are having difficulty to suffer regular humiliation in the classroom. Teacher appraisal is another way of opening the classroom door. Supportive appraisal schemes should improve standards of classroom management.
>
> *The Elton Report* (1989) pp. 76, 78

Questions for peer support

1. What forms of peer/collegiate support are available to me?
2. What use do I make of peer support?

3. In what ways would I want:
   - My colleagues to realistically support me?
   - My year level co-ordinator, head of department/faculty head?
   - My principal?
4. Are there people here I can count on for assistance in any circumstance? Who?
5. In what ways are my skills, abilities, contribution (and 'worth') acknowledged and affirmed?
6. Am I in a position to give collegiate support in a formal, semi-formal, ad hoc way? How will I go about it?
7. What professional advice and guidance do I receive? From whom? Do I regard that advice and guidance as authoritative and trustworthy?

A more general question for senior staff is, 'In what ways can we develop a culture of support in our school for staff and also students?'

CHANGE AND STRESS

Whenever we embark on changes in our teaching and management practices we put ourselves under pressure. I believe most teachers want to address both stress management and professional development, yet the very act of changing (improving, modifying, fine-tuning) our practice itself creates stress — natural stress. Embracing a new repertoire means thinking, practice, approximating, trial and error, re-evaluation. It means taking a journey from conscious ineffectiveness towards conscious effectiveness (Rogers 1992b). The effort applied in that 'journey' is of itself *naturally* stressful; there is a discomfort zone we go through before the 'new' skills become familiar and comfortable. This is normal.

While we want to moderate our stress level in concert with an increase in skill repertoire, our stress level may increase for a period of time.

Some teachers I've trained (on site, in schools) get quite annoyed that the new skills are making them feel worse. 'I might as well go back to shouting, arguing, acting from my guts....at least I felt better!' This is true — even though the behaviour of the teacher may be dysfunctional, the teacher feels better than when he tries the new skill.

Change in our practice won't happen overnight. Reflection fine-tuning and practice (and where possible discussion with our peers) are the right ingredients with a healthy self-forgiveness where we fail.

The key is to hang in there. You will only do this, of course:

- if you see a need (and use) for the new (different) skill repertoire;
- if you value the purpose of using these approaches as distinct from other approaches in discipline;
- if you see some success in terms of the objectives;
- and if you get support from colleagues taking a similar journey.

Watch out for cynics; you know, the ones who Oscar Wilde said, 'know the price of everything and the value of nothing.' And remember, 'The secret of success is the ability to survive failure' (Noel Coward).

Minimising stress

Teaching is a stressful occupation. Teachers have to meet deadlines, time, workload and marking pressures. In the classroom they juggle several demands at the same time: teaching to a wide ability range, discipline and encouragement, curriculum organisation, marking — day after day. They also have to report meaningfully to parents. These are only a few of the natural stresses of our job.

Stress is related to the demands of the job, the perception we hold about our role, the students and their behaviour and the degree of support we receive from our peers. Realistic attitudes will help. If I say to myself children *must* do what teachers say, must do precisely as they're told, or that I must be able to control children's behaviour; if I hold to these beliefs persistently and dogmatically I'm unlikely to be able to maintain a sense of balance. A student has only to say, 'I'm not going to do this', 'This work is boring', 'Can't make me!' and a significant mismatch is 'caused' between reality and one's belief. The cause of stress is, therefore, more than merely the stressful events we face in our job.

While we can't merely *control* the child's responses we can manage them in a way that will minimise uncooperative attitudes. We can control our own beliefs, perceptions and reactions to the students in such a way as to minimise the effects of stress.

More realistic and functional beliefs would be:

- 'It's *preferable* that children respect me and my role.'
- 'I'll work in such a way that makes it likely that children will respect me, but if for some reason they don't, it's not the end of the world!'

- 'I can cope. I'm not going to become a screaming heap because of a belief that says they must perform in the way I say they should.'
- 'When I fail I'll recognise it for what it is — a failure. It doesn't make me a failure. It means I've failed — what can I learn from it?'

Some of the skills discussed in this book when tried will see some failure. That's OK and normal. We can allow for it and eschew the silly attitude that says, 'I must get it right first and every time!'

Also a judicious sense of humour will enable us to laugh off, and laugh at, some of the student behaviours and some of our stressful situations without getting them out of perspective.

The eight-out-of-ten principle

Teaching, like any job, has its 'bad' days. What job (banged up on a wet day with twenty-five plus students) wouldn't? Especially when our own life is under some stress and strain. The flat tyre, headache, hassles at home, the worksheets you forgot to prepare.... If on those days we 'blow it' it is wiser to forgive ourselves for natural failure and fallibility and move one. We need to let the students know, too, on the 'bad' days that we're feeling uptight — students are quite forgiving. A brief word will often help. I recall one day when I had a bad headache (I'd come in as a 'martyr'). Having told them I'd probably not be my kind, calm self, today, Rob, a bit worried, came over and said, 'Mr Rogers, wanna drink of water?'

If we get any of the approaches in this book right on an eight-out-of-ten average, we've done well. That leaves us a two-out-of-ten fallibility ratio!

Conclusion

Place twenty-five (or more) students (compulsorily) in a room, often too small with inadequate furniture (for size and comfort), add poor lighting and heating, and you are bound to get some disruptive behaviour. Add to the environmental conditions the fact that teachers pick up the widest range of human behaviour and have to manage behaviour for a third of a student's working day — clearly the measure of a teacher's discipline and management task is significant, even onerous.

To deal effectively, and positively, with behaviour in schools such that the goals of mutual self-discipline and respect for mutual rights are realised is no mean feat. It takes planning, skills, goodwill and plenty of collegial support.

Can I encourage you to reflect on your language in the discipline and management context? When we engage students in addressing their behaviour and its effect on others we rely on communication skills; nowhere is communication more taxing than when we are annoyed by students' disruptive behaviour, or where their behaviour is affecting the rights of others to learn or feel safe or to be treated with respect.

People outside our profession have little idea how draining our teaching role is, they often use perceptual models of the 1950s. It is different today in that the social context has changed, children are keenly aware of their rights and more vocal about them.

Yet students still need leadership, guidance and positive discipline. They still need a secure structure in which to balance rights and responsibilities and they still need rules. They need teachers not just for teaching and learning but to help and support them in their journey towards self-discipline, behaviour accountability and respect for *mutual* rights.

It is highly desirable that a school should set out a school-wide plan for achieving those aims and professionally developing staff within positive discipline practices.

It is also important to develop a strong collegiate support culture in our schools to promote emotional well-being, structural forums for problem solving and opportunities for elective feedback on our professional practice. If this book can support these aims it will have achieved its purpose.

Bibliography

Barrish, H. H., Saunders, M. and Wolf, M. M. (1969) Good behaviour game: Effects of Individual Contingencies for Group Consequences on Disruptive Behaviour in the Classroom, in *Journal of Applied Behaviour Analysis*, Vol. 2, pp. 119–24.

Bernard, M. (1990) *Taking the Stress Out of Teaching*, Collins Dove, Melbourne.

Brown, D., Reschly, D. and Sabers, D. (1974) Using Group Contingencies With Punishment and Positive Reinforcement to Modify Aggressive Behaviour in a 'Head-Start' Classroom, in *Psychological Record*, Vol. 24, pp. 491–6.

Coopersmith, S. (1967) *The Antecedents of Self-Esteem*, Freeman, San Francisco.

Dalton, J. (1985) *Adventures in Thinking: Creative Thinking and Co-operative Talk in Small Groups*, Thomas Nelson, Melbourne.

De Bono, E. (1986) *Conflicts: A Better Way to Resolve Them*, Penguin, Harmondsworth.

Doyle, W. (1986) Classroom Organization and Management, in M. C. Whitrock (ed) *Handbook of Research on Teaching*, 3rd edn., Macmillan, New York.

Dreikurs, R. (1968) *Psychology in the Classroom: A Manual for Teachers*, 2nd edn, Harper and Row, New York.

Dreikurs, R. (1971) *Social Equality: The Challenge of Today*, Contemporary Books Inc., Chicago.

Dreikurs, R., Grunwald, D, and Pepper, F. (1982) *Maintaining Sanity in the Classroom*, 2nd edn, Harper and Row, New York.

Elton Report (1989) *Discipline in Schools, Report of the Committee on Inquiry*, Her Majesty's Stationary Office, London.

Glasser, W (1986) *Control Theory in the Classroom*, Harper and Row, New York.

Glasser, W (1991) *The Quality School: Managing Students without Coercion*, Harper and Row, New York.

Kounin, J (1971) *Discipline and Group Management in Classrooms*, Holt, Rhinehart and Winston, New York.

Kyriacou, C. (1981) Social Support and Occupational Stress Among School Teachers in *Educational Studies*, Vol. 7, pp. 55–60.

Kyriacou, C. (1986) *Effective Teaching in Schools*, Basil Blackwell, Oxford.

Kyriacou, C. (1987) Teacher Stress and Burnout: an International Review in *Educational Research*, Vol. 29, no. 2, June, pp. 146-52.

Maultsby, M. C. (1977) Basic Principles of Intensive Rational Behaviour Therapy: Theories, Goals, Techniques and Advantages in *Twenty years of Rational Therapy*, Institute for Rational Living, New York.

Nelson, J. (1987) *Positive Discipline*, Ballantyne Books, New York.

Powell, J. (1976) *Fully Human, Fully Alive*, Argus Communications, Illinois.

Robertson, J. (1989) *Effective Classroom Control: Understanding Teacher-Pupil Relationships*, 2nd edn, Hodder and Stoughton, London.

Rogers, W. (1989) *Making a Discipline Plan*, Thomas Nelson, Melbourne.

Rogers, W. (1989) *Decisive Discipline: Every Move You Make, Every Step You Take*, Institute of Educational Administration, Geelong, Victoria (a video-learning package).

Rogers, W. (1991a) *You Know the Fair Rule*, Longman, Harlow.

Rogers, W. (1991b) Dealing with Procrastination, *Topic 2*, Issue 6, NFER.

Rogers, W. (1992b) Peer Support: Peers Supporting Peers, *Topic 1*, Issue 7, NFER.

Rogers, W. (1992b) *Supporting Teachers in the Workplace*, Jacaranda Press, Milton, Queensland.

Russell, D. W., Altmaier, E. and Van Velzen, D. (1987) Job Related Stress: Social Support and Burnout Among Classroom Teachers in *Journal of Applied Psychology*, May, Vol. 72, no. 2, pp. 269-74.

Rutter, M., Maughan, B., Mortimer, P. and Ouston, J. (1979) *Fifteen Thousand Hours: Secondary Schools and Their Effects on Children*, Open Books, London.

Sacks, O. (1990) *Awakenings*, Picador, London.

Seligman, M. (1992) *Learned Optimism*, Random House, Milson's Point, Aus.

Smith, P.K. and Thompson, D. (1991) *Practical Approaches to Bullying*, David Fulton, London.

Wheldall, K. (ed.) (1992) *Discipline in Schools: Psychological Perspectives on the Elton Report*, Routledge, London.

Wragg, J. (1989) *Talk Sense to Yourself: A Programme for Children and Adolescents*, ACER, Hawthorn.

Index

More Books on Education Management

The following pages contain details of a selection of other titles on Education Management. For further information, and details of our Inspection Copy Service, please apply to:

Northcote House Publishers Ltd, Plymbridge House, Estover Road, Plymouth PL6 7PZ, United Kingdom. Tel: Plymouth (0752) 695745. Fax: (0752) 695699. Telex: 45635.

A selection of catalogues and brochures is usually available on request.

Beyond the Core Curriculum

Co-Ordinating the Other Foundation Subjects in Primary Schools

EDITED BY
MIKE HARRISON

To help schools to meet the needs of the National Curriculum, primary teachers are required increasingly to act as consultants to their colleagues in particular subjects. This task of curriculum co-ordination often demands a new range of skills from teachers whose expertise may, hitherto, have been confined mainly to classroom teaching.

This practical book helps those charged with leading their school's staff in: Geography, History, Physical Education, Information Technology, Music, Art and Design, Technology, and Religious Education to develop their subject knowledge, network with others and find ways to influence colleagues to ensure that their subject is taught imaginatively and coherently in the school.

Written by a team of primary specialists this book offers invaluable advice and support to headteachers, teachers and students for whom the co-ordination of the foundation subjects in primary schools is an area of growing interest and responsibility.

The Editor, Mike Harrison, is Director of the Centre for Primary Education in the University of Manchester. He has worked as a primary teacher and a headteacher, leads primary pre-service education and is currently running inter-LEA courses for primary co-ordinators. He is known nationally for his courses on education management for prospective primary deputy heads. He is co-author of *Primary School Management* (Heinemann, 1992).

The ten co-authors are all primary experts in their fields, many running twenty-day training courses for primary co-ordinators in their subjects.

Paperback, 192 pages, tables.

Evaluating the Primary School

A Practical Guide to Effective Evaluation

BRIAN HARDIE

There has been an increasing emphasis on evaluation in schools since the 1988 Education Act. Schools now need to know if they are meeting the requirements of the National Curriculum and the expectations of the community and parents looking for evidence of measurable success for their children.

This practical handbook provides step-by-step guidance on the evaluation process and offers specific advice on a range of techniques and methods for both whole school and classroom evaluation. It will serve as an invaluable reference and as a source of practical help to all parents, governors, teachers and educationalists involved in evaluating their schools.

Brian Hardie MA DLC is Senior Lecturer in Education Management at the Crewe & Alsager Faculty of the Metropolitan University of Manchester. He specialises in primary school management and is the author of *Marketing the Primary School* (Northcote House, 1991).

Paperback, approx 144 pages, illustrated. (in preparation)

Managing Stress in Schools

A practical guide to effective strategies for teachers

MARIE BROWN & SUE RALPH

Managing stress is a growing problem for teachers in schools as they seek to meet the increasing demands of the National Curriculum, local management of schools (LMS), and the rising expectations of parents understandably wanting quantifiable examination results for their children approaching the highly competitive labour or higher education markets for the first time.

Based on sound psychological theory and research the emphasis of this book is, throughout, on practical solutions to teacher stress. Its sound analysis and realistic advice will enable teachers and those responsible for staff development both to identify the causes of stress, and to formulate a whole school policy for its management within the school.

Sue Ralph and Marie Brown both teach in the University of Manchester School of Education. They lecture and research in Educational Management and Administration, and Education and the Mass Media, and run inservice courses for teachers and other professionals. They have researched and published extensively on the effects of stress on teachers.

Paperback, 176 pages (approx), tables. (in preparation)

Managing the Primary School Budget

An Introduction for Teachers and Governors

BRENT DAVIES & LINDA ELLISON

With the framework of the Local Management of Schools firmly in place, heads, staff and governors need to turn their attention to its implementation at the local school level.

This practical guide begins by establishing the key dimensions of LMS and reviews the nature of income and expenditure in the primary school. It moves on to a consideration of the way in which budgeting fits into school management development planning and examines the role of staff and governors in the process.

The book then adopts a step-by-step approach using a case study school to demonstrate how to go through the three key stages of budgetary review, planning and implementation. This will provide primary schools with a practical framework enabling them to manage their new-found financial responsibilities.

Brent Davies BA MSC teaches in the Centre of Education Management, Leeds Metropolitan University and is an LMS adviser to a large number of local education authorities. He has provided LMS management training for over 1000 primary heads in differing LEAS. He is the author of *Local Management of Schools* and a large number of articles on delegated finance. He is joint author with Linda Ellison of *Education Management for the 1990s*.

Linda Ellison MSc is a Senior Lecturer in charge of Education Management at Leeds Metropolitan University. She is extensively involved with programmes of senior management training, particularly for heads and deputies in primary schools. She has also been involved in the provision of staff development on LMS in a variety of LEAS. She is joint author with Brent Davies of *Education Management for the 1990s*.

'...a simple, step-by-step guide through what can be a bewilderingly dense forest.' *Times Educational Supplement*.

Paperback, 128 pages, tables.

Marketing the Primary School

An Introduction for Teachers and Governors

BRIAN HARDIE

Schools have always had an eye on their 'reputation' and standing within the local community. However, open enrolment and competition for pupil numbers following the 1988 Education Reform Act have put a much greater value on the relationship which schools need to have with both parents and pupils. Now, in order to increase — and even maintain — pupil numbers, schools will be under much greater pressure to market themselves effectively. The author, who has been running courses in marketing and reputation management for primary school heads, shows how the primary school can be successfully promoted, stretching precious resources to make the most of contacts with the local community. Contents: Preface, the school in its marketplace, reputation management, marketing the school, meeting the customer, the prospectus and other communications, handling the media, further reading, useful addresses, glossary, index.

Brian Hardie MA DLC is a Senior Lecturer in Education Management at Crewe & Alsager Faculty of the Metropolitan University of Manchester, and runs courses in marketing and reputation management for primary school Heads. He is the author of *Evaluating the Primary School* (Northcote House, 1994).

'... tells heads how to think the unthinkable... sound advice about things that good schools should have been doing for years...' *Times Educational Supplement.*

'The book works, as a handbook to be used and returned to as different activities are needed. The context and priority are right...the ingredients for the successful mix are right...the focus and presentation of the advice are simple and sharp.' *NAGM News.*

Paperback, 144 pages, illustrated.

Local Management of Schools

BRENT DAVIES & CHRIS BRAUND

Written by two consultants in this important field, this book meets the pressing need for an introductory handbook to help governors, teachers and parents get to grips with major new responsibilities now becoming mandatory. Readable and practical, the book spells out the new legislation and what it means, the new financial structure in secondary and primary schools, the new role of Head teachers and governors in delegated school management, and what it means for the future. Complete with case studies and suggested management exercises.

> 'The nine main chapters, each dealing with a different aspect, are easy to read, comparatively jargon-free, and gave me a very good overview of LMS.... This reference book will justify a place in any educational establishment because of its accessible information and advice.' *Junior Education*.

> 'Well favoured by the brevity/practicality formula, written with governors and parents in mind as well as teachers. It is strong on illustrative yet simple graphics and tables and does not shirk the consequences of falling numbers.' *Times Educational Supplement*

Paperback, 96 pages, tables.

The School Library

ELIZABETH KING MA ALA

Written by a former Chairperson of the School Library Association, this book appraises the role of school libraries in a changing world — a world in which new ideas, new technology and new initiatives (and financial cutbacks) present a special challenge for the professional.

> 'A stimulating appraisal of the role of the school library in a changing educational world of cutbacks, information technology and educational reform.' *Junior & Middle School Education Journal*.

> 'A masterly account of how to organise a school library. . . Anyone reading this will feel invigorated... [to ensure] that all school children have access to a working school library resource centre.' *School Library Association*.

Paperback, 112 pages, illustrated.

The School Meals Service

NAN BERGER OBE FHCIMA

The importance of the school meals service is becoming better recognised today, following greater interest in diet and health, and the advent of privatisation and what it means for standards of service in the educational system. This new book meets the longstanding need for an introduction to—and defence of—the School Meals Service. Expert, readable and forthright, it reviews key health and management issues for everyone having a professional interest in children's welfare, from head teachers and governors to catering managers and educational administrators.

Contents: Foreword, acknowledgements, the beginnings, what the service is and does, the structure of the service, training, nutrition, organising the production of school meals, the stigma of the free school meal, the competition, the problem of midday supervision, the economics of the School Meals Service, the effects of the Education (No. 2) Act 1980, the role of the Government, the future of the School Meals Service, appendices (organisations, statistics, notes on Scotland and Northern Ireland), chronology, bibliography, index.

> 'Informative, thought-provoking and controversial.' *Lunch Times*. 'Maori-style cooking has not, to my knowledge, been much practised by our own School Meals Service, though no doubt ungrateful children would have their parents believe otherwise. The kind of folklore perception of school dinners is tackled in Nan Berger's School Meals Service. There is much more to the book than this, however, for it is a thorough and well documented history of the meals service, starting with its origins in the last century and moving on to recent traumas of privatisation and closure.' *Times Educational Supplement*.

Nan Berger OBE FHCIMA is former Editor of the *National Association of School Meals Organisers Handbook* and *Hospitality* magazine.

Paperback, 144 pages, illustrated.